Mandala
Technical Coloring Books

Copyright: Published in the United States by Janice Perrine
Published January 2017
ISBN-13: 978-1542642002
ISBN-10: 1542642000

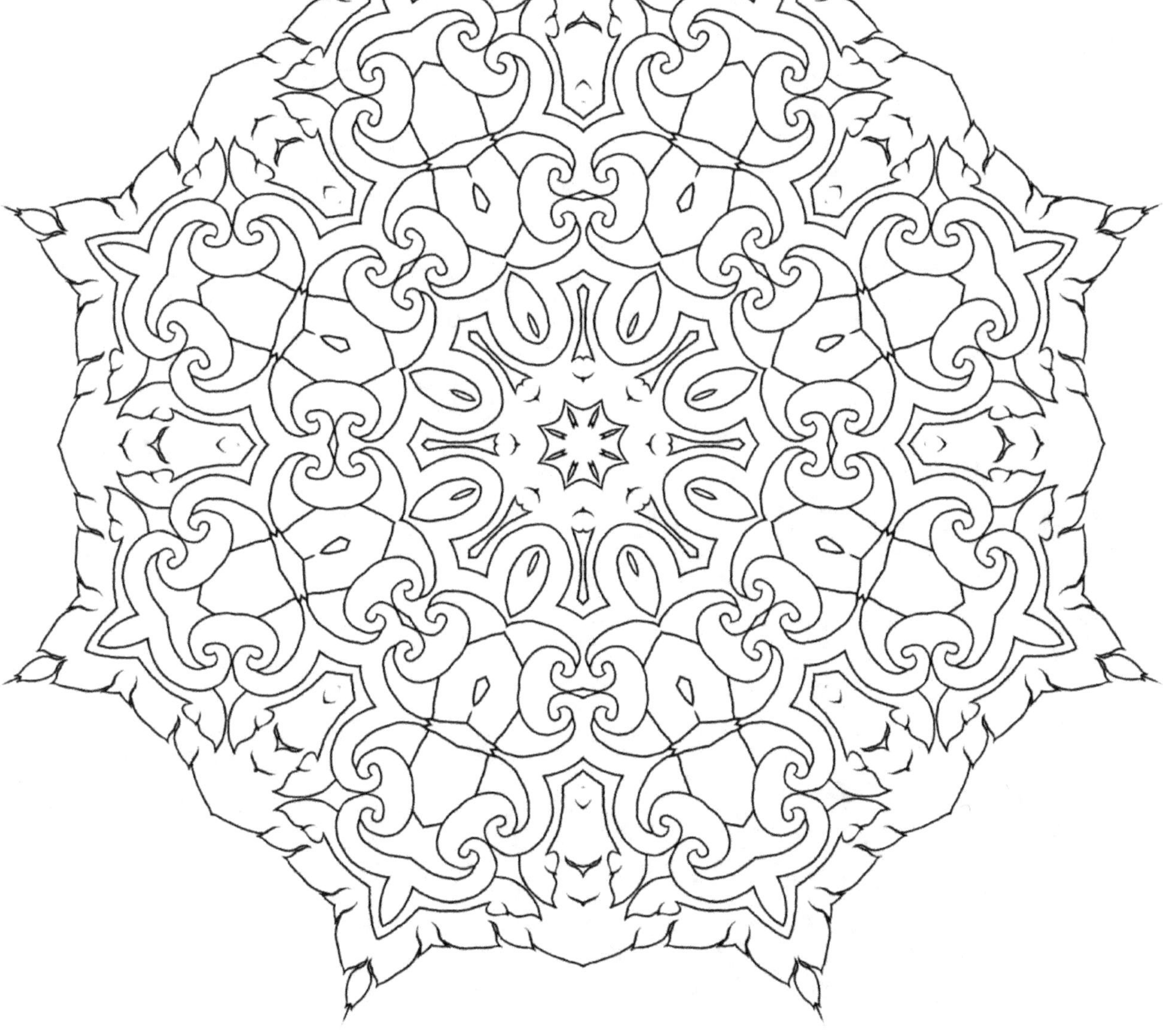

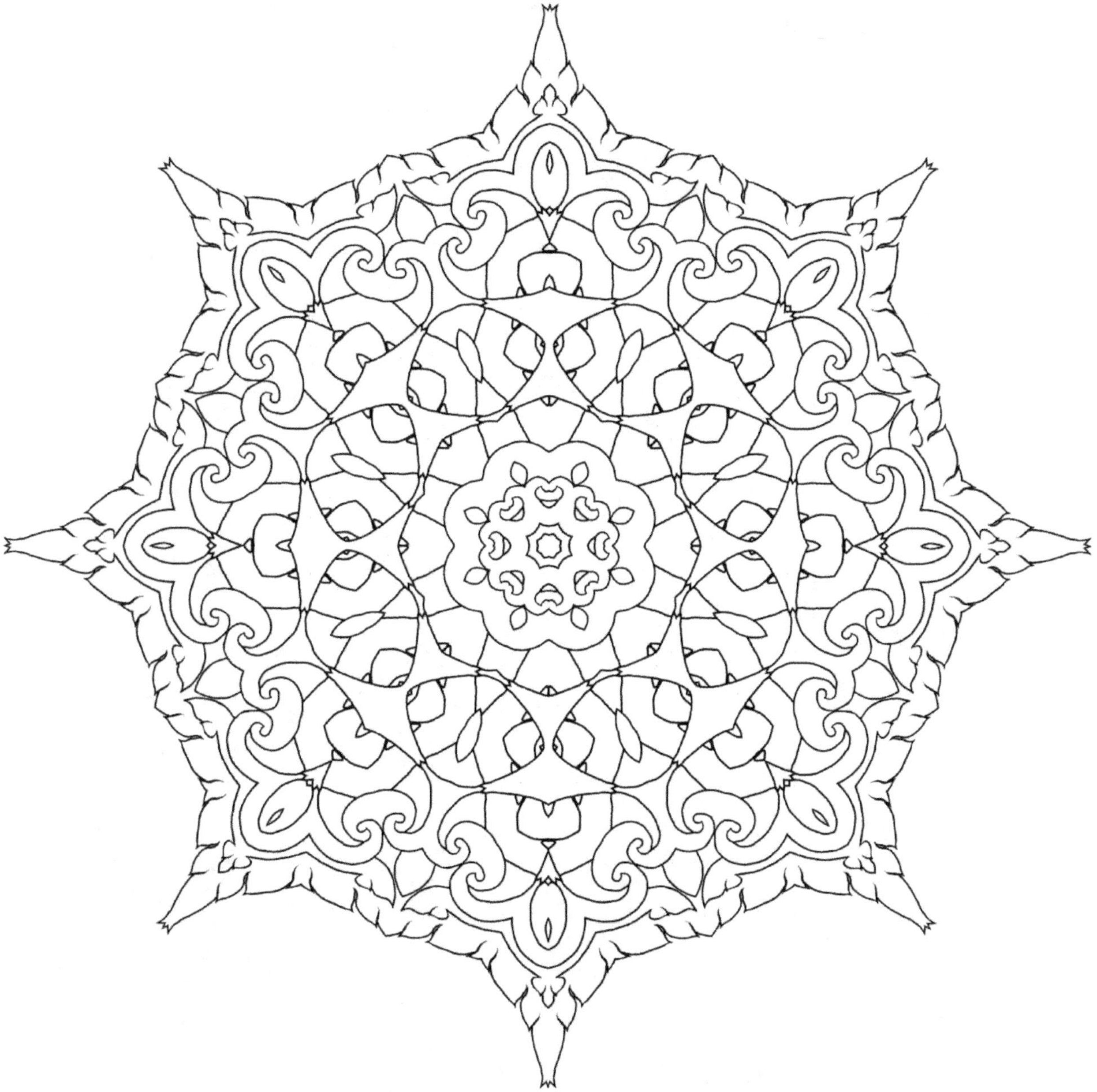

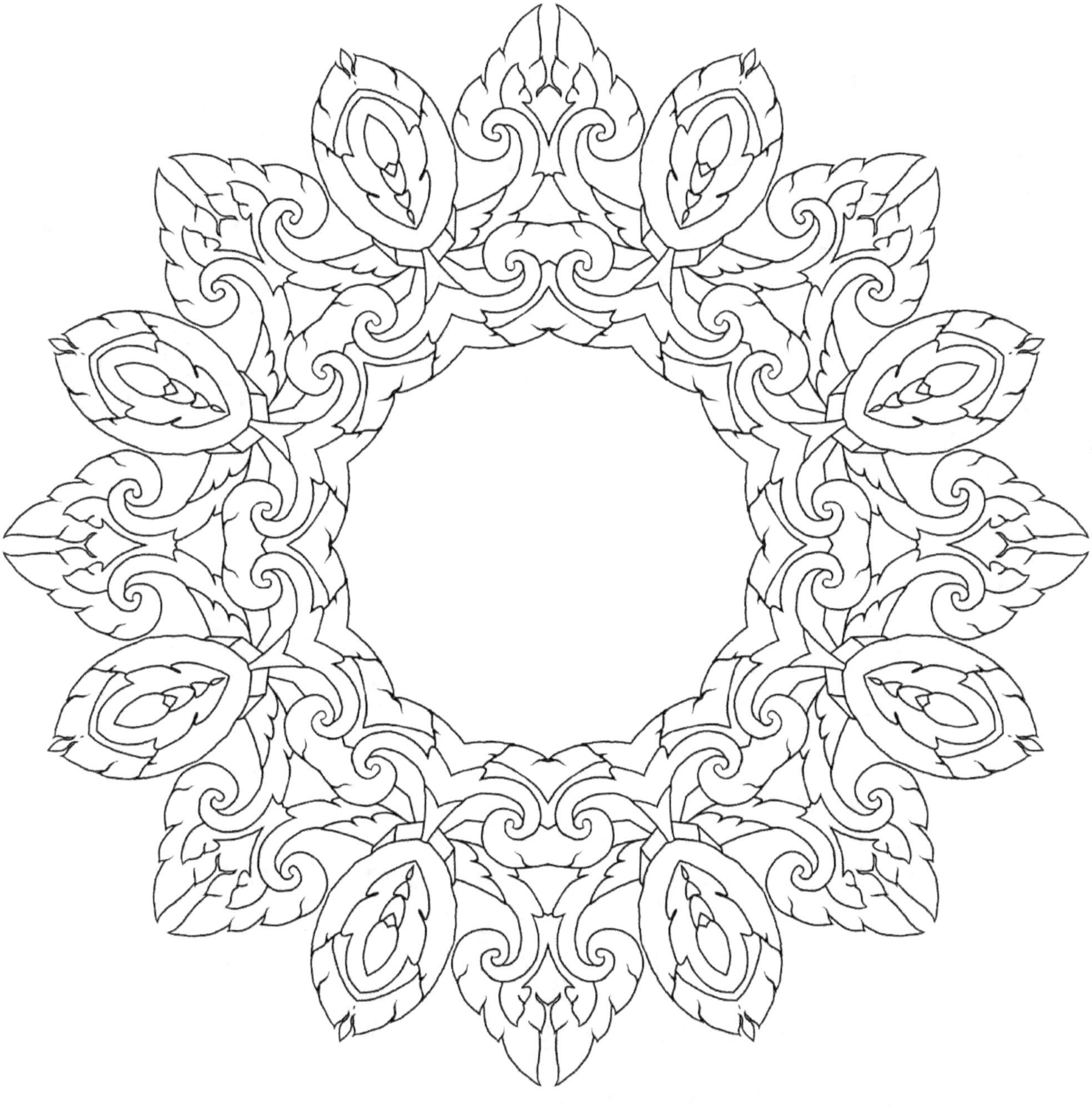

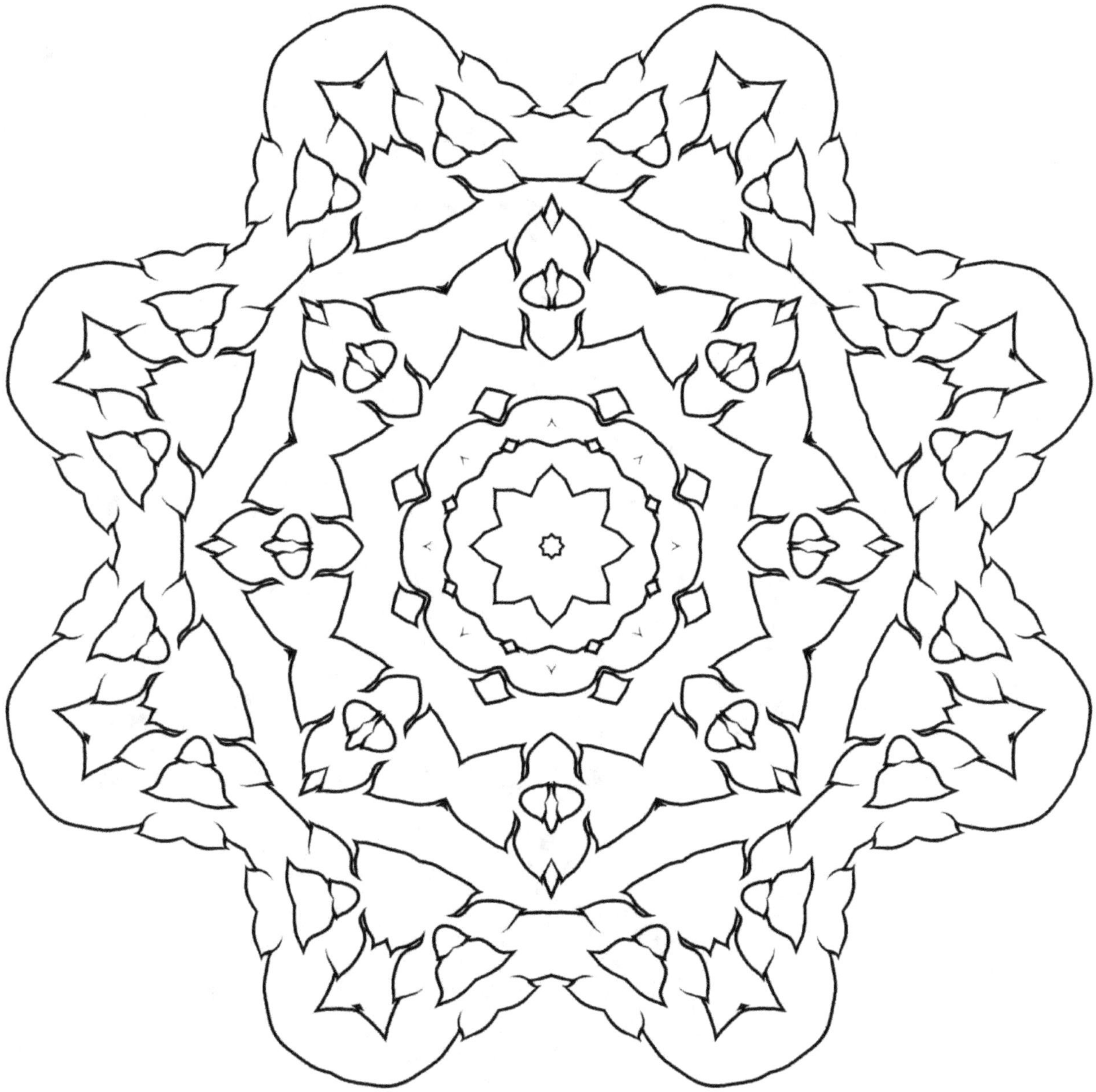

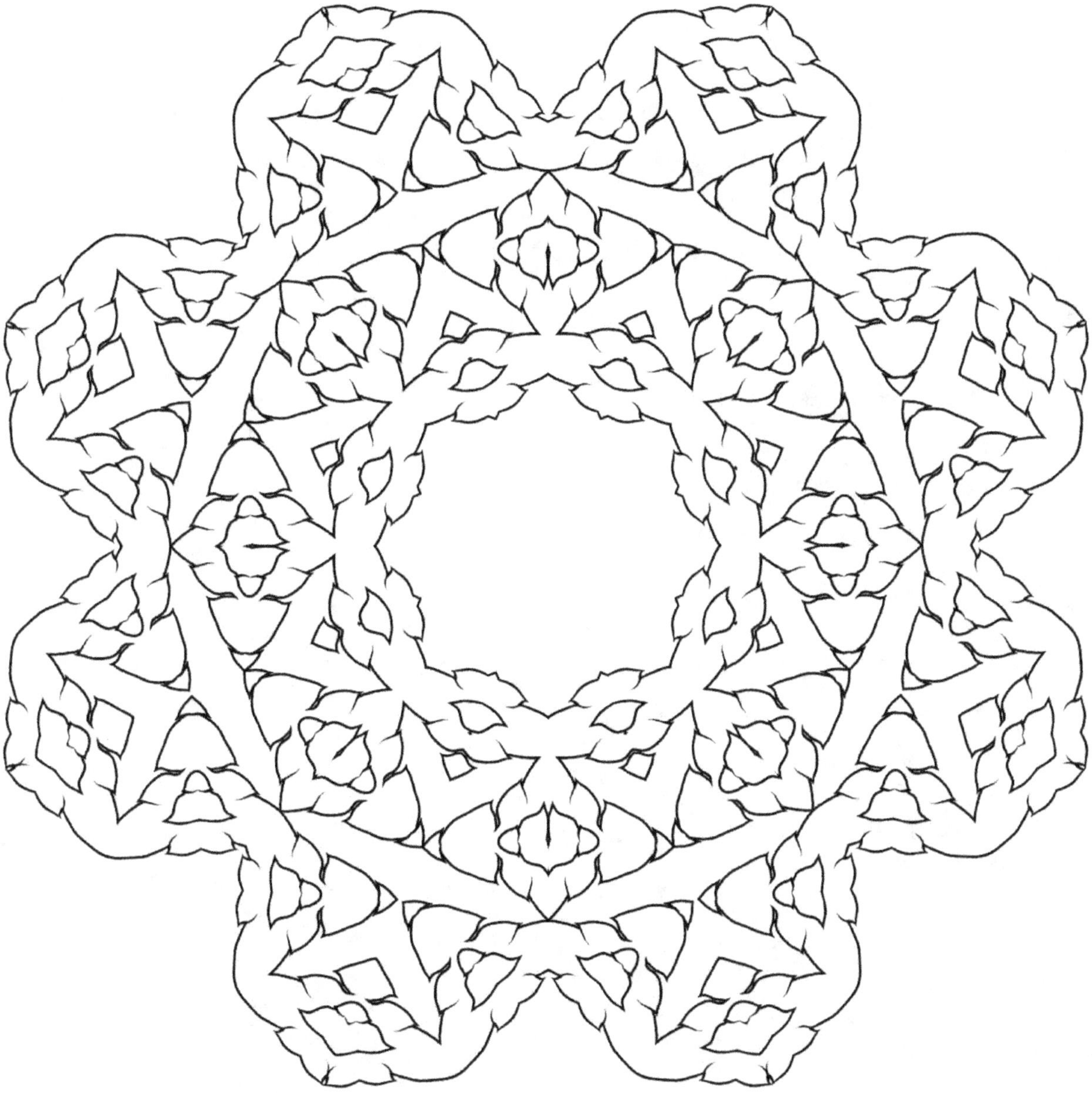

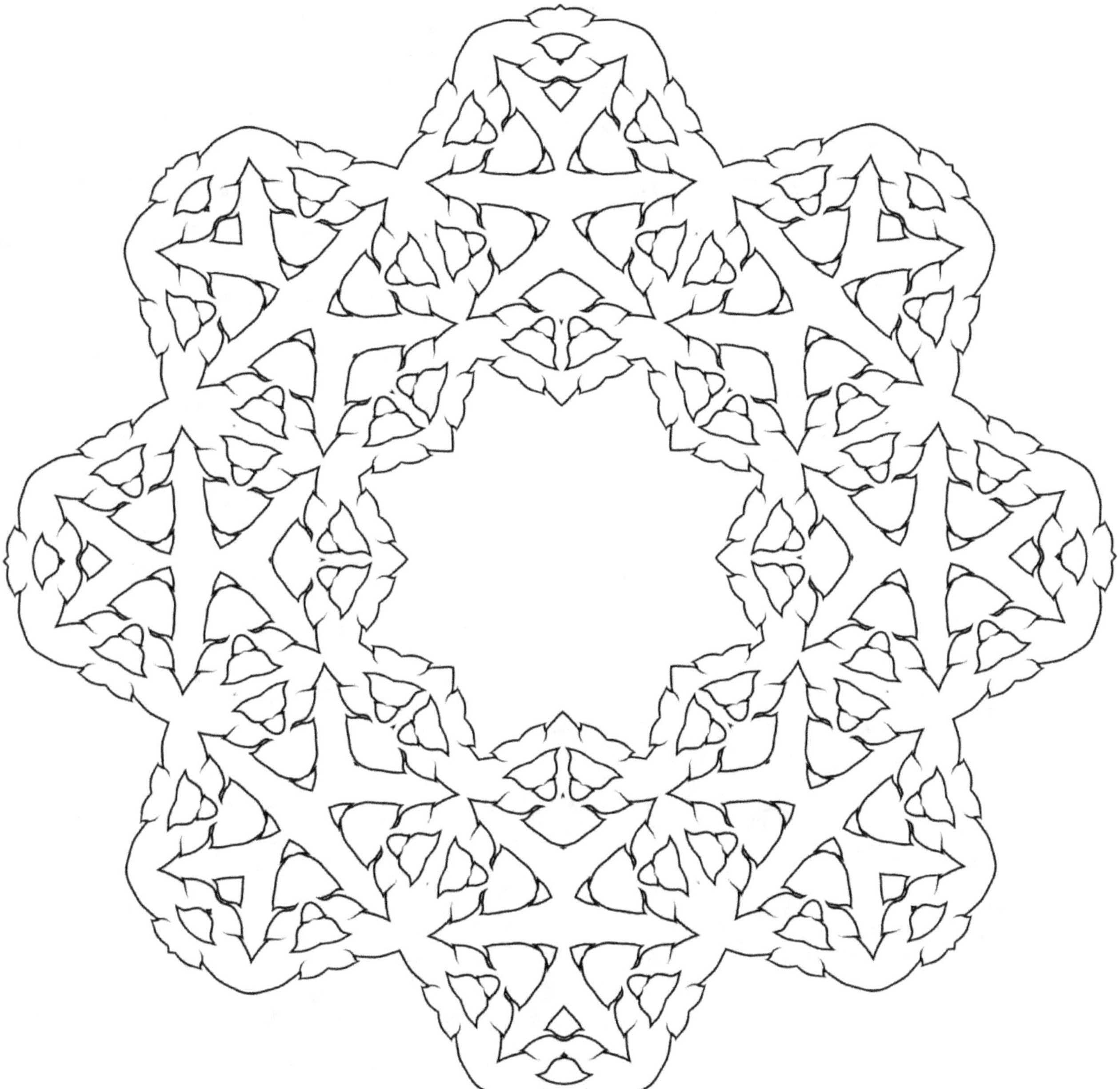

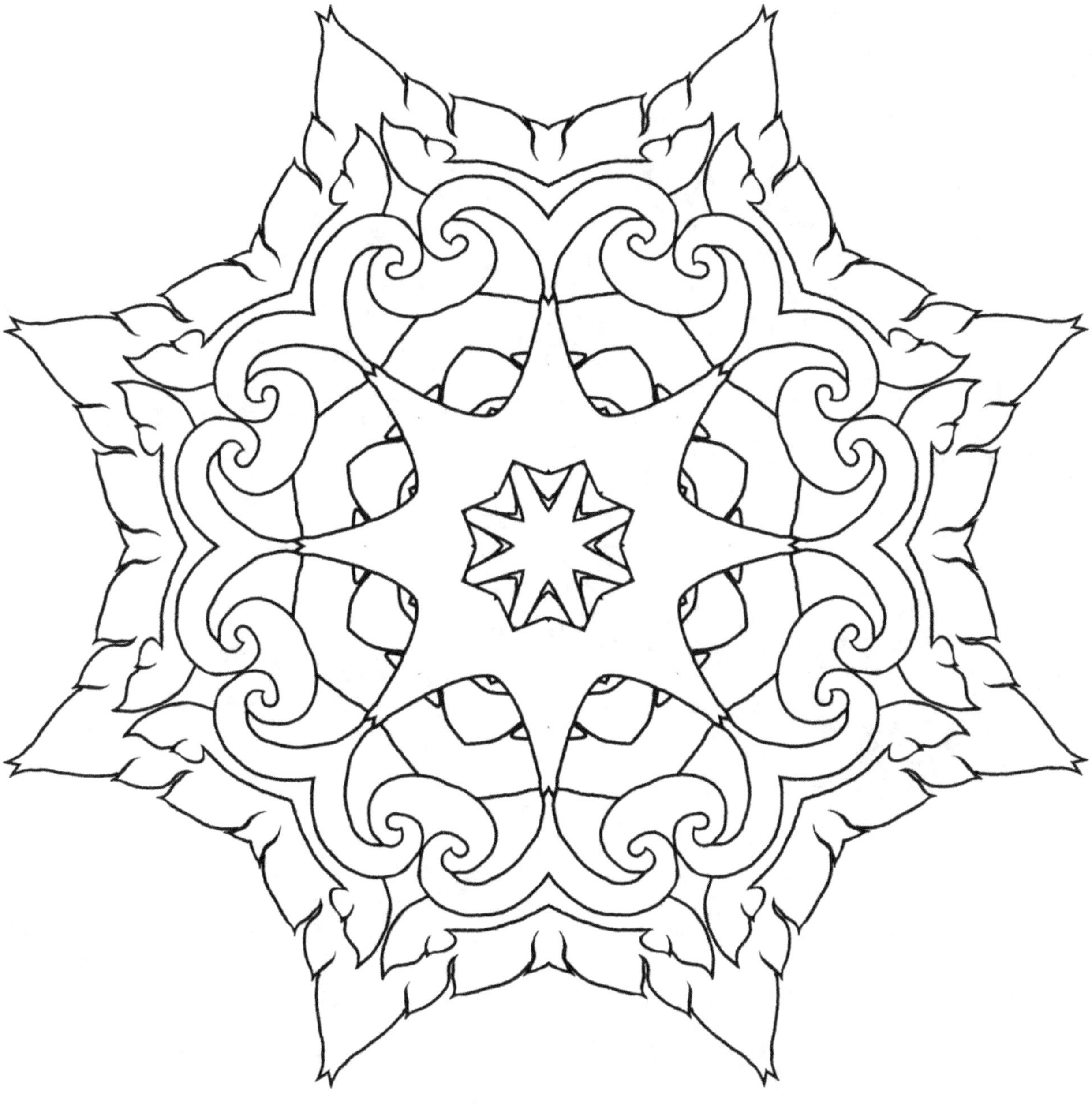

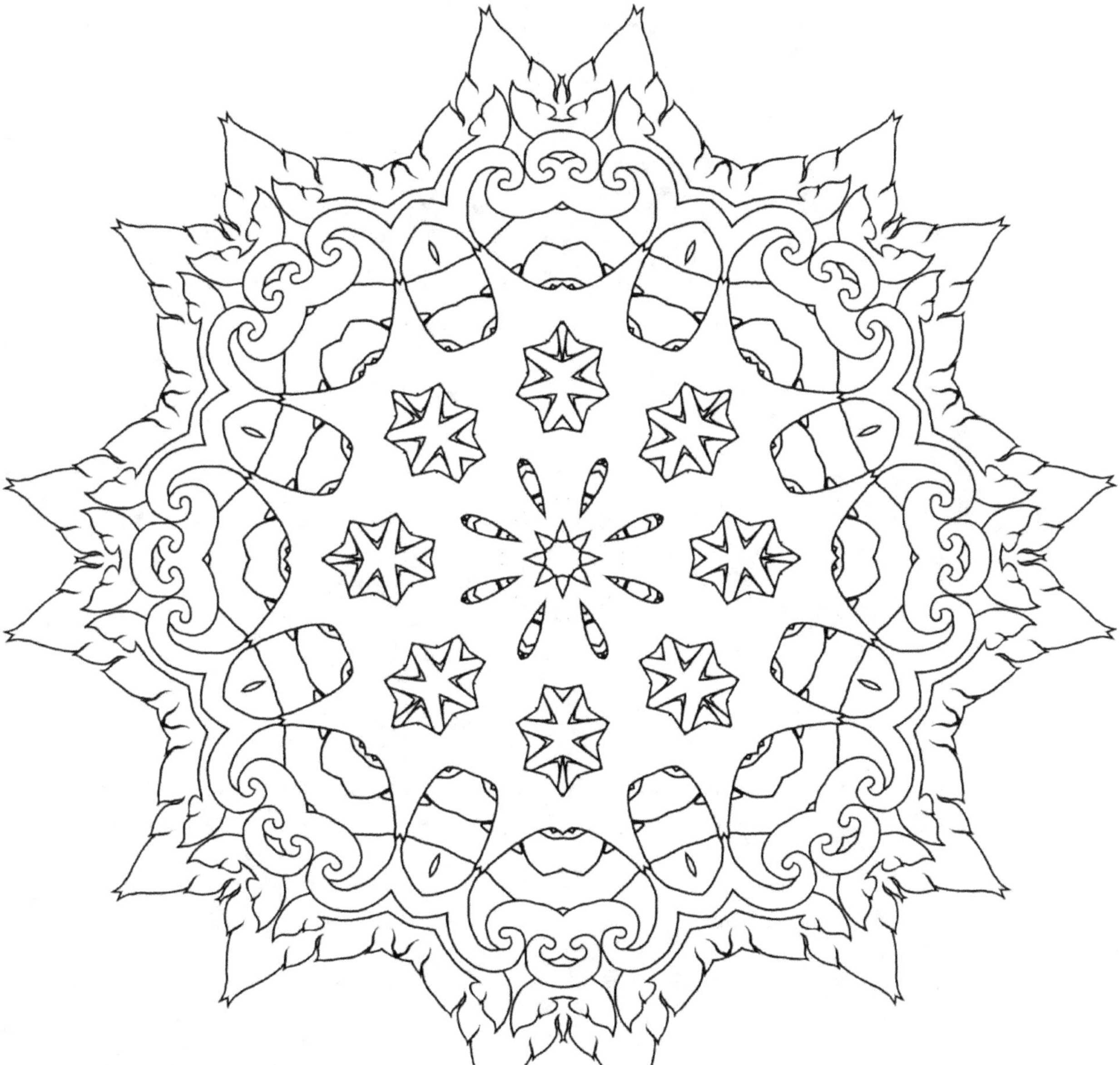

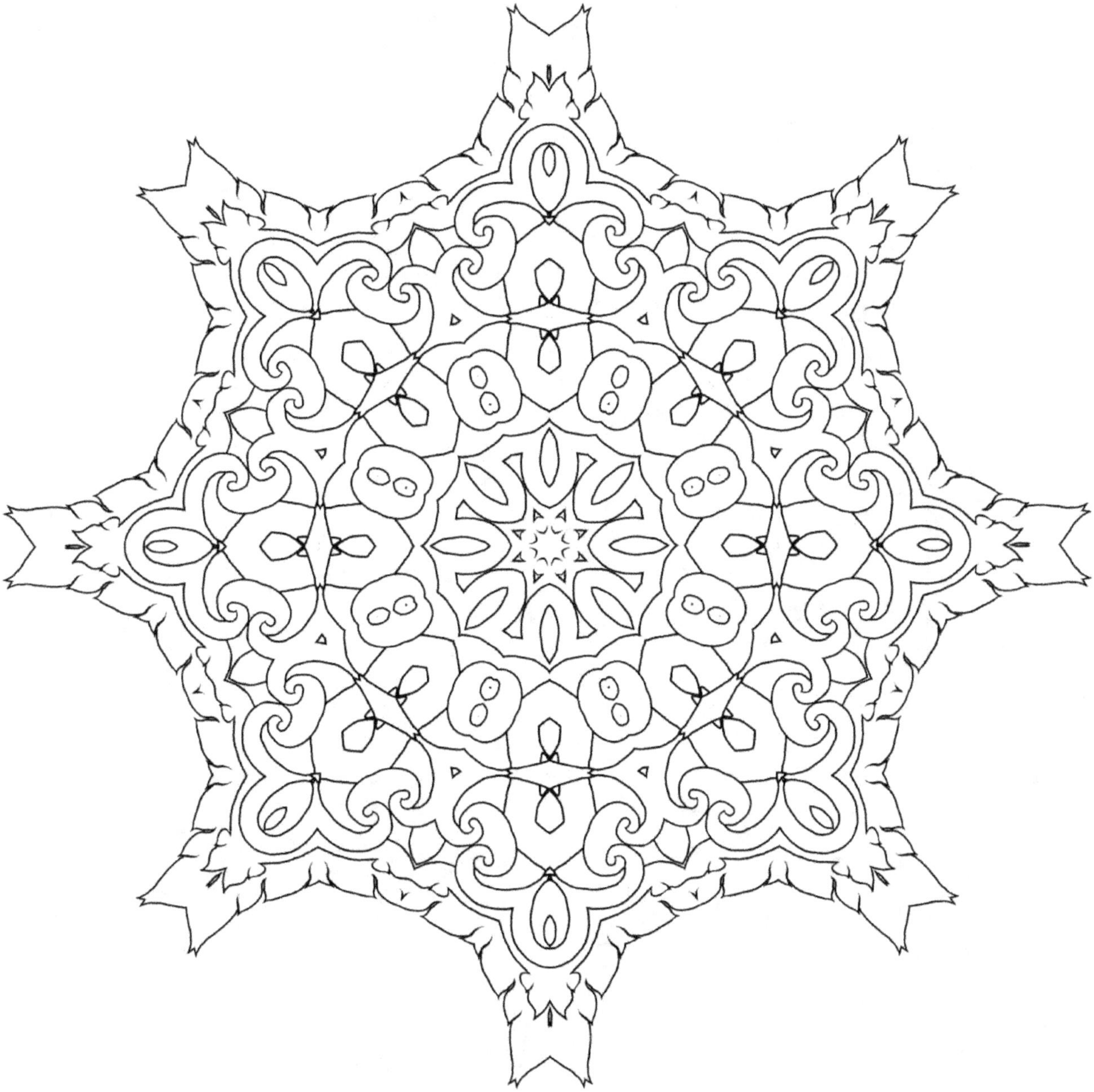

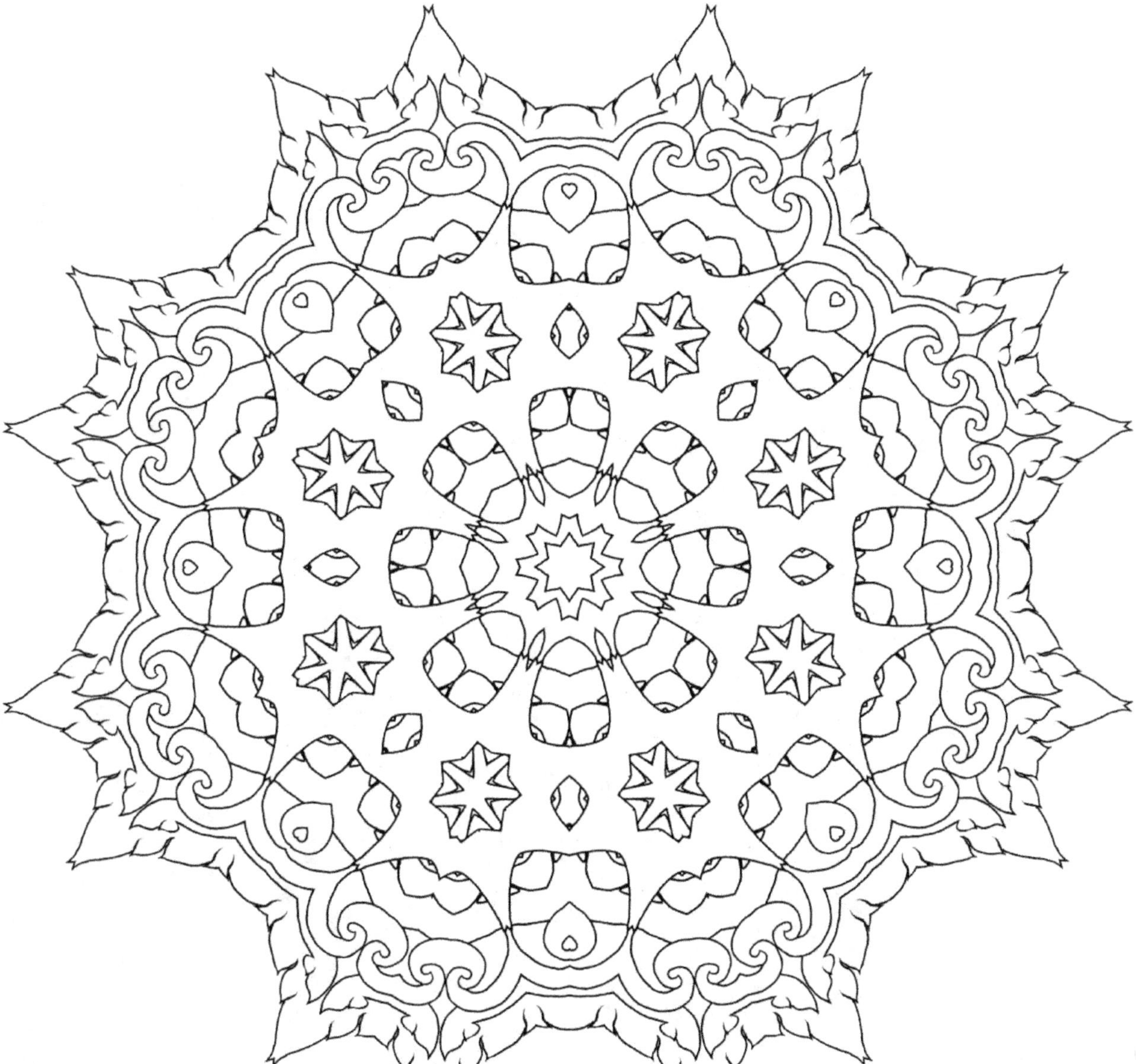

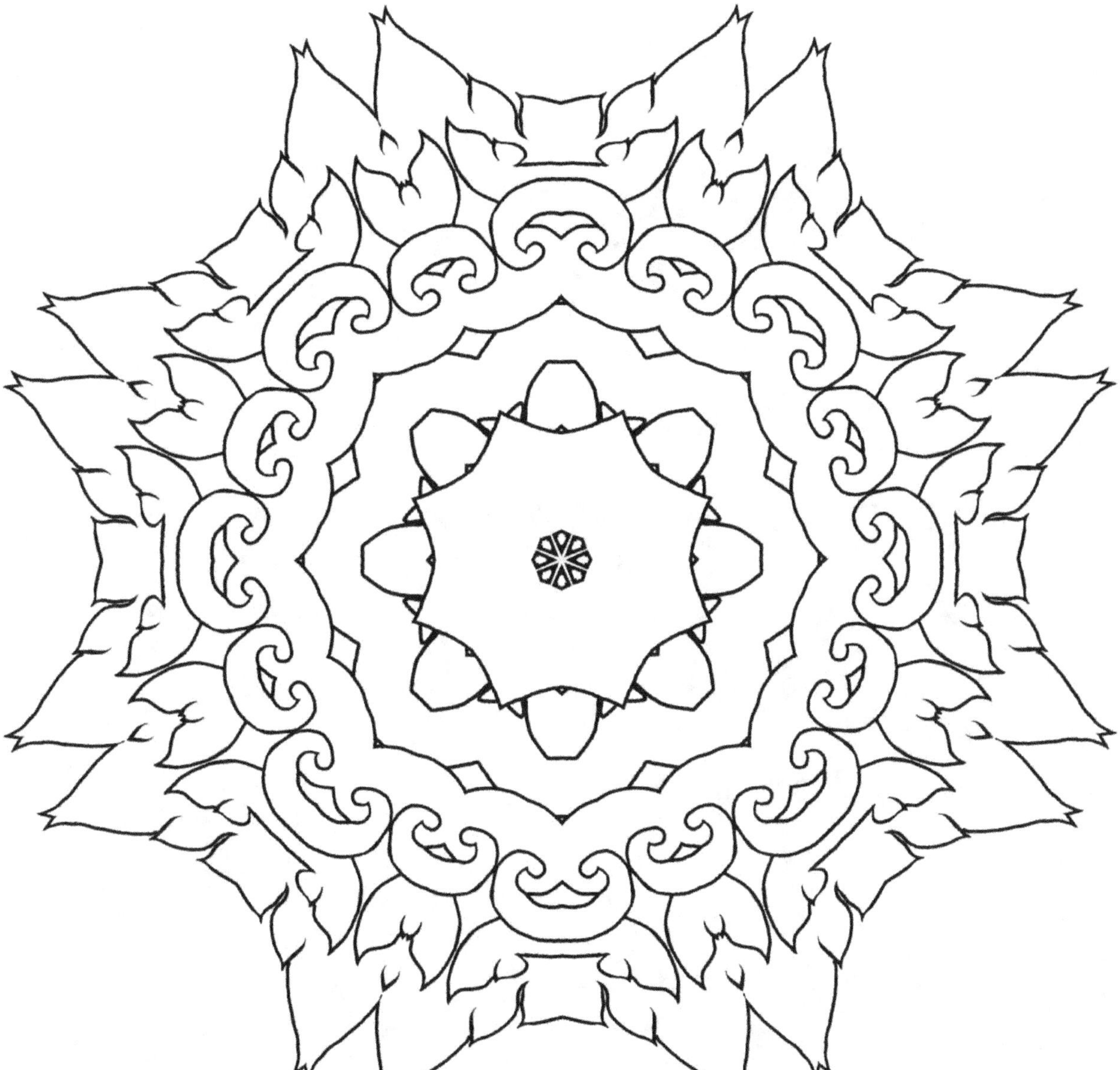

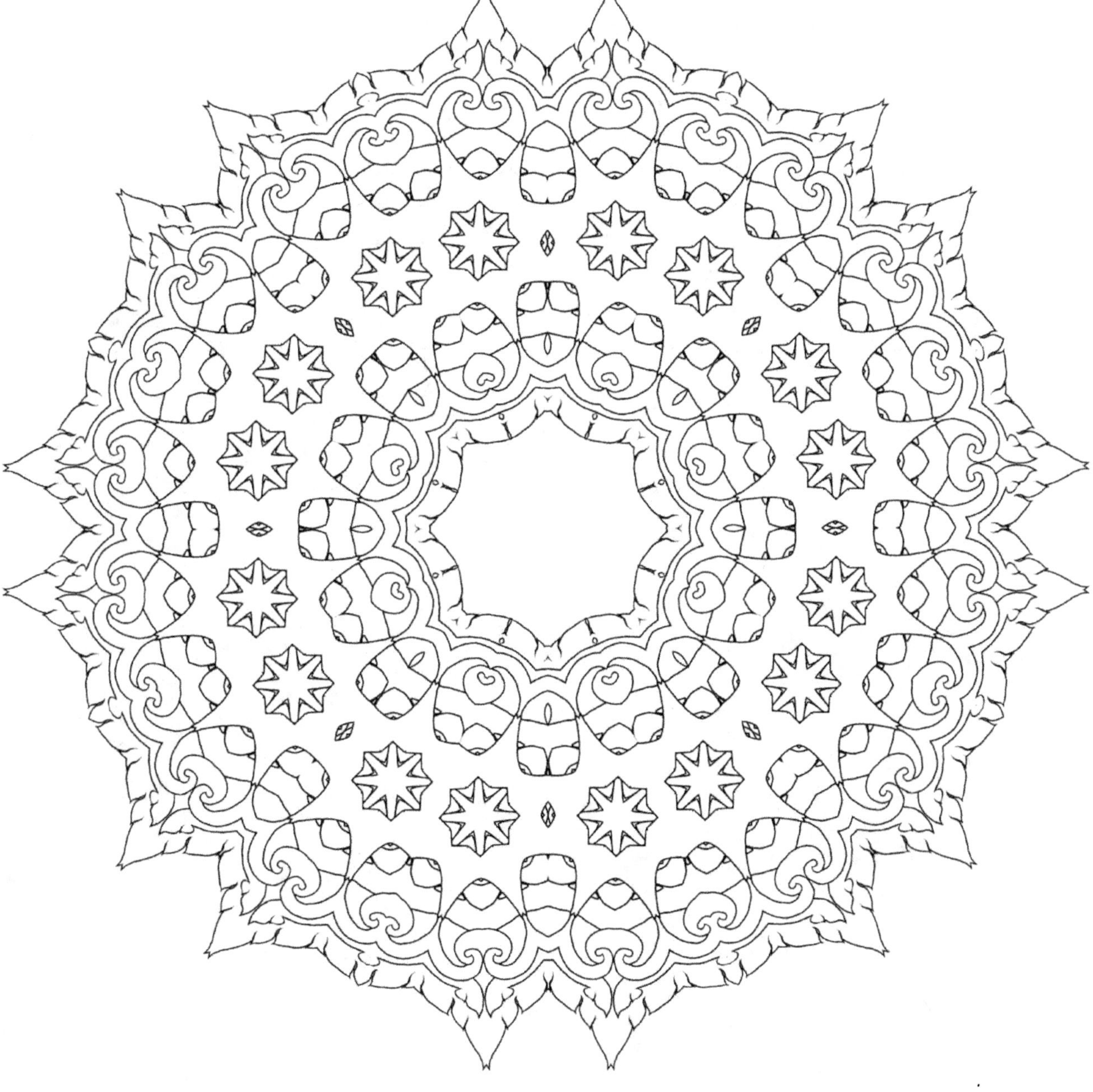

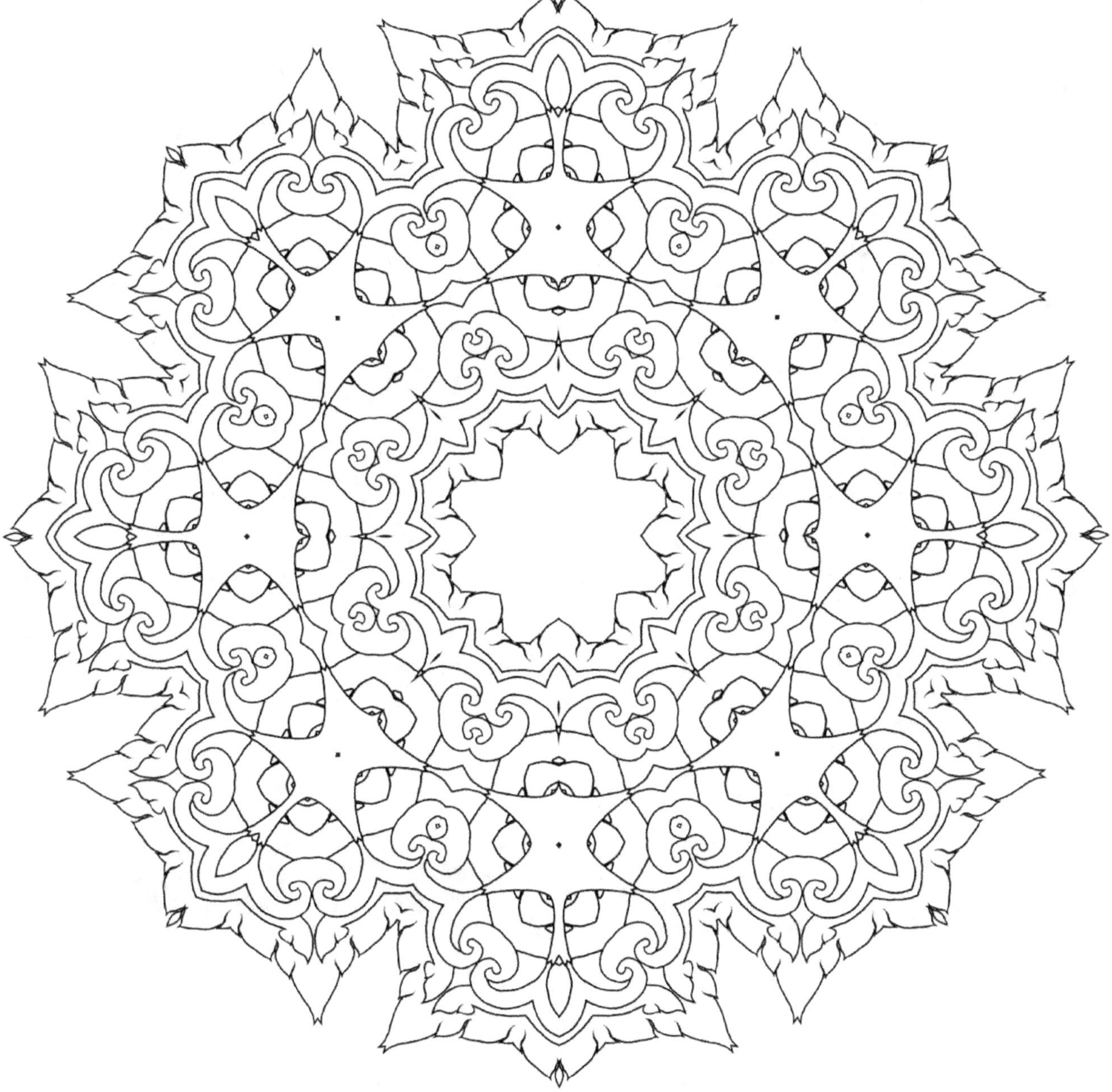

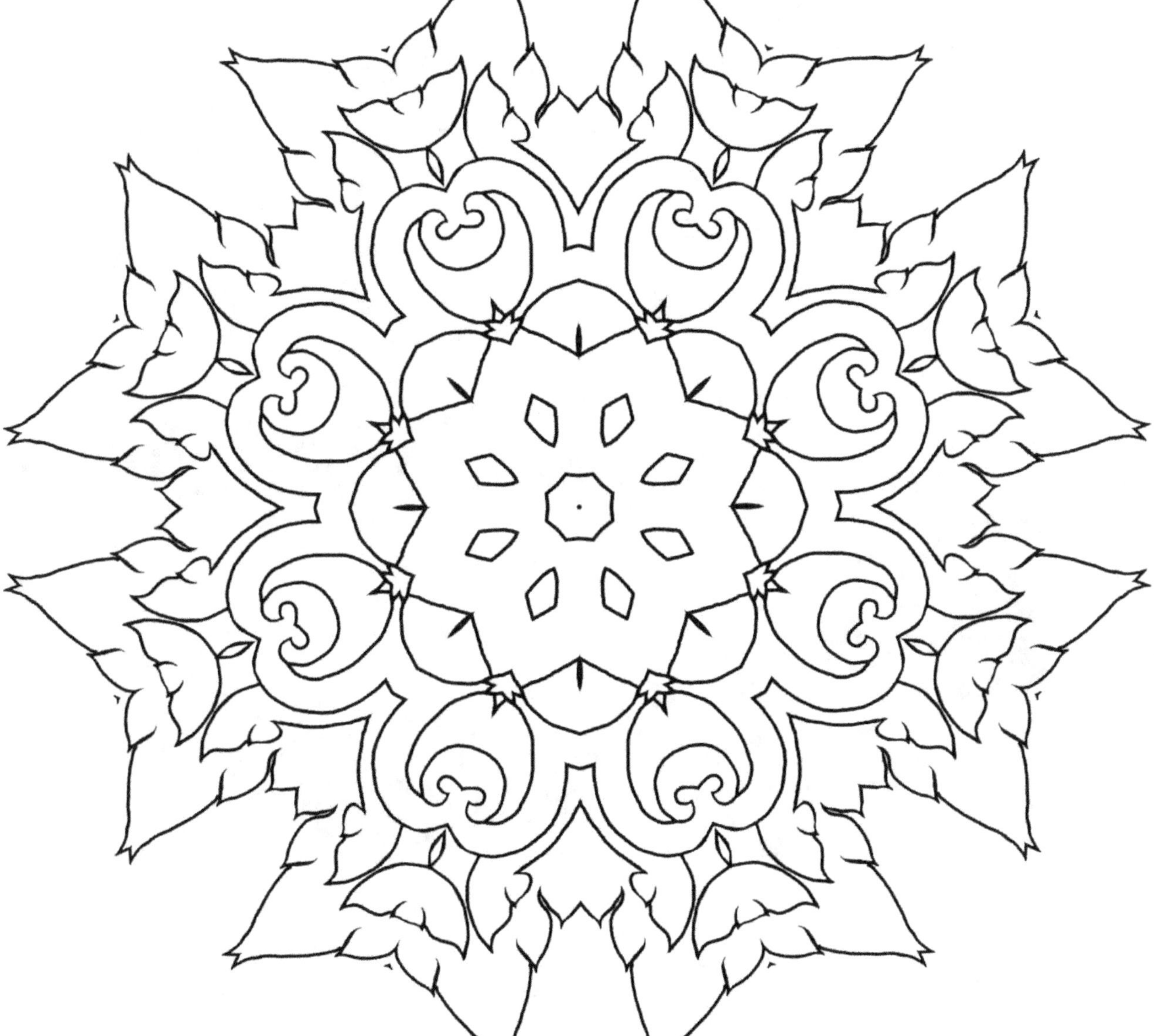

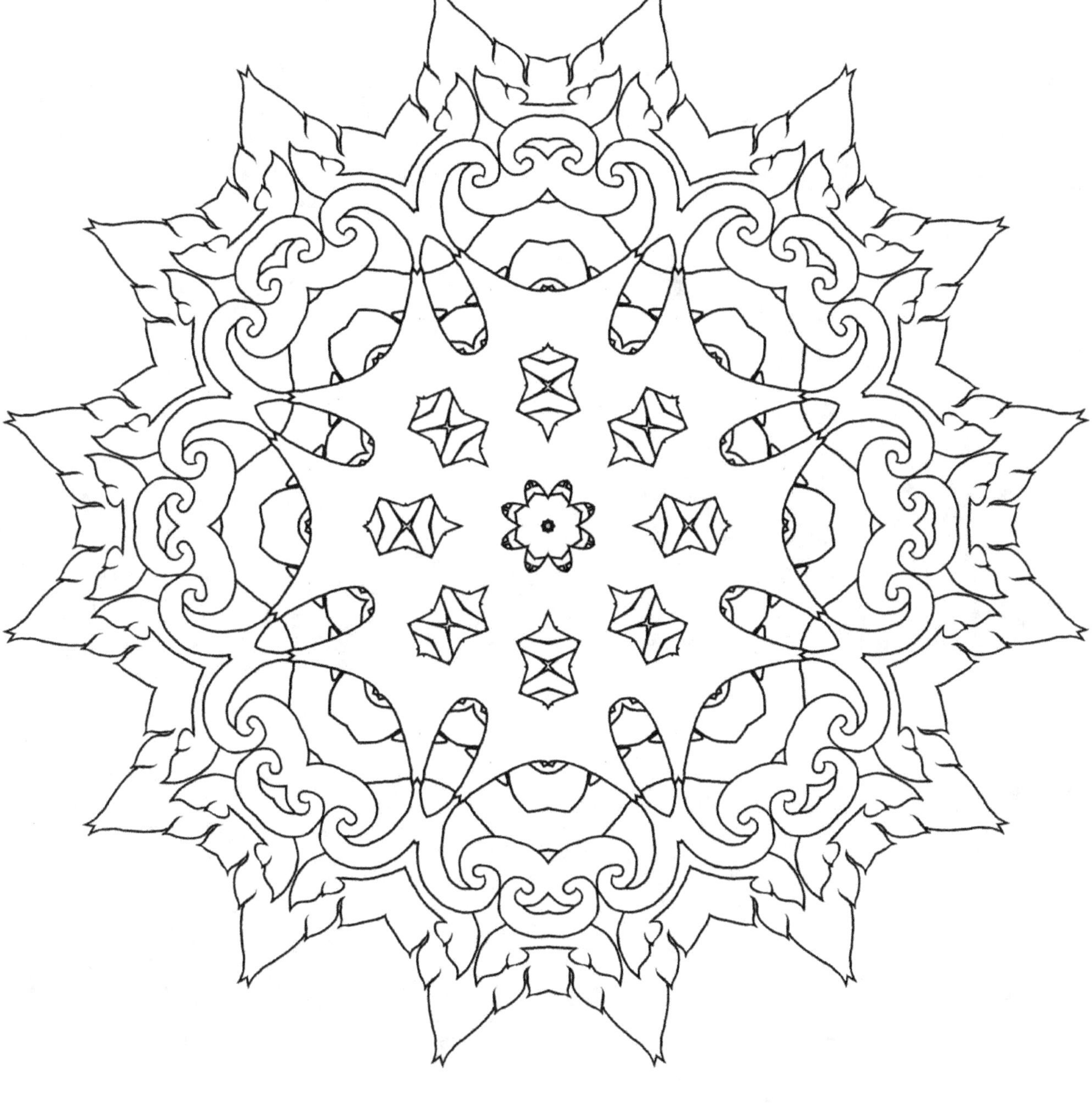

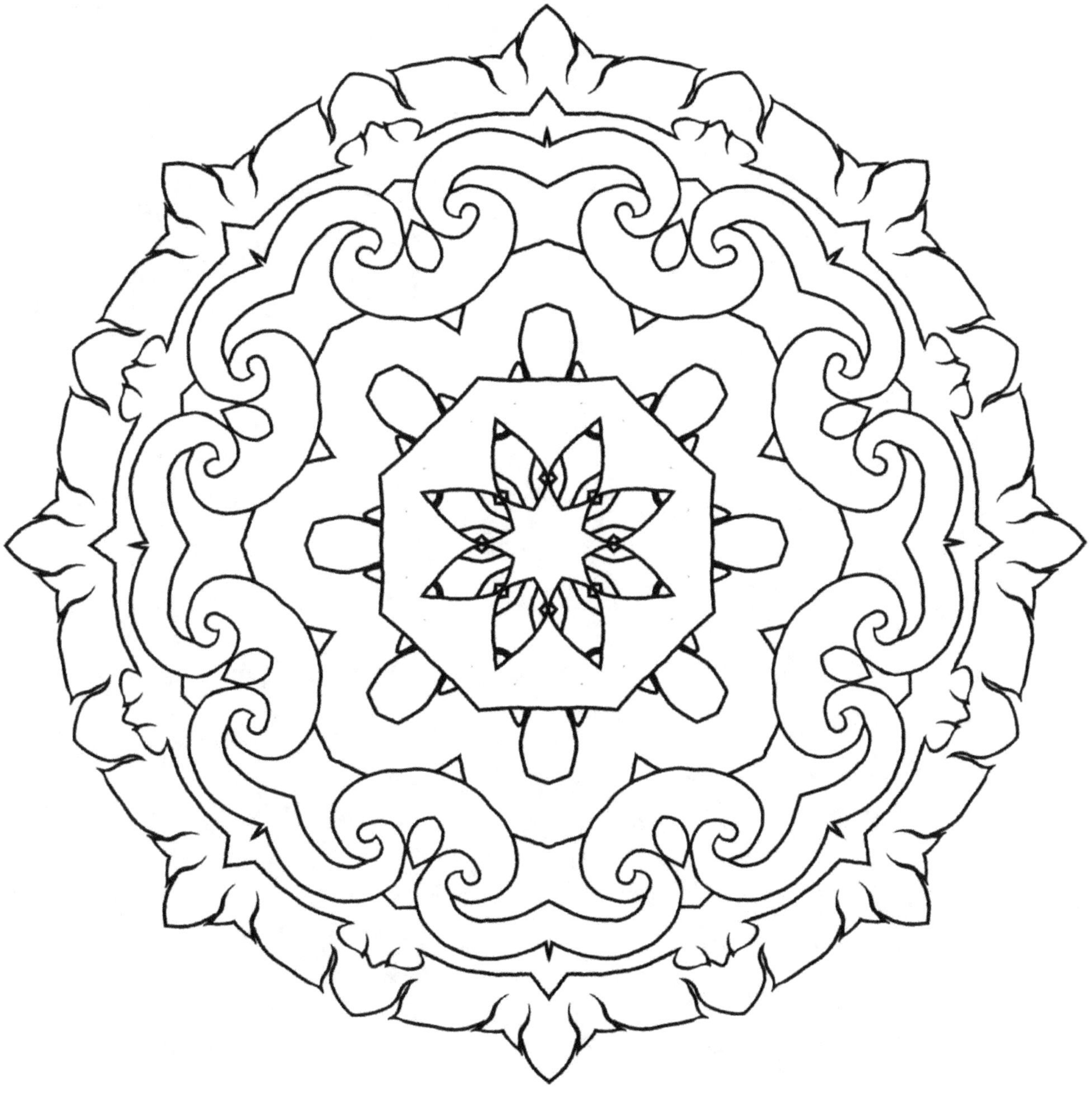

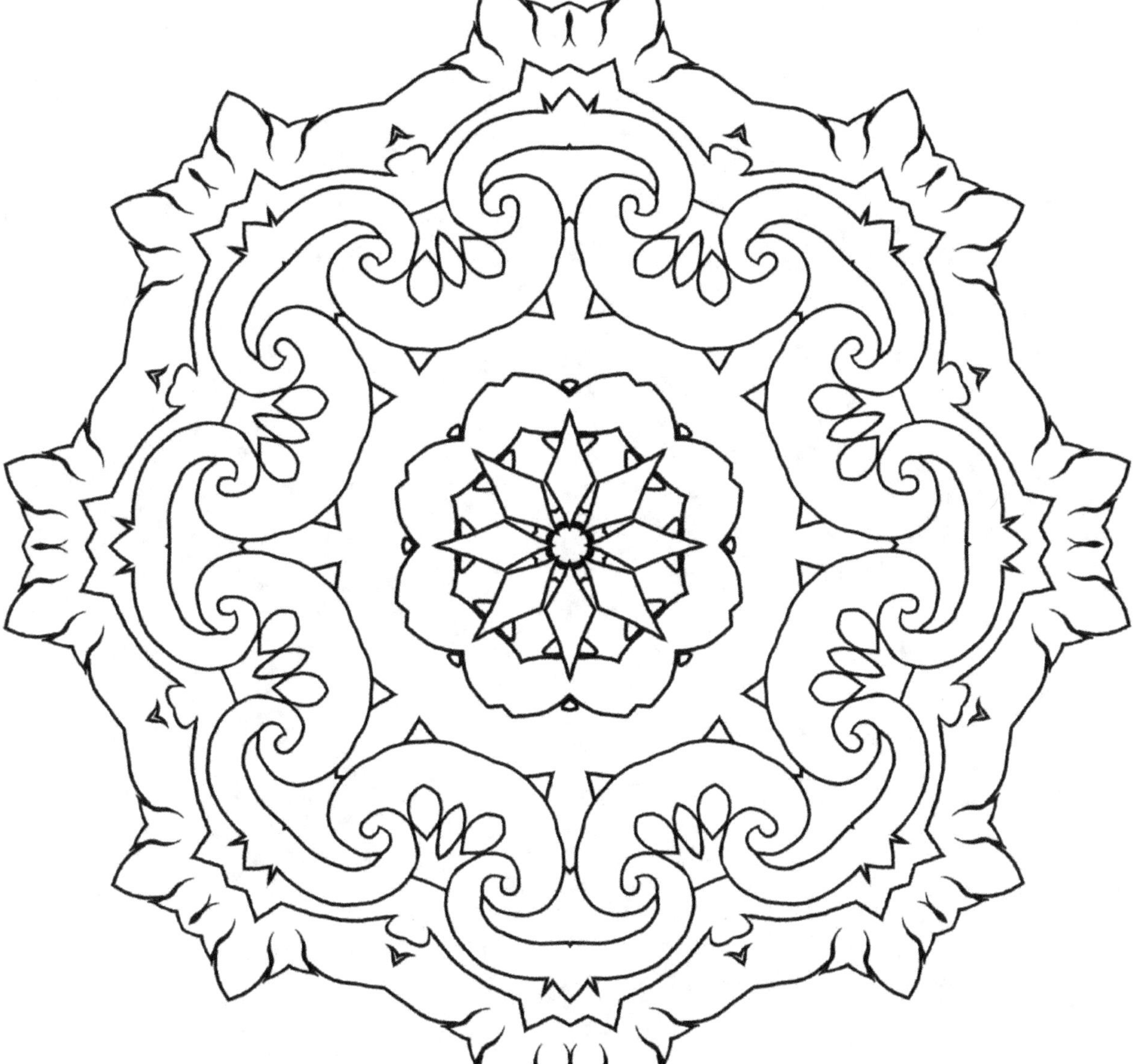

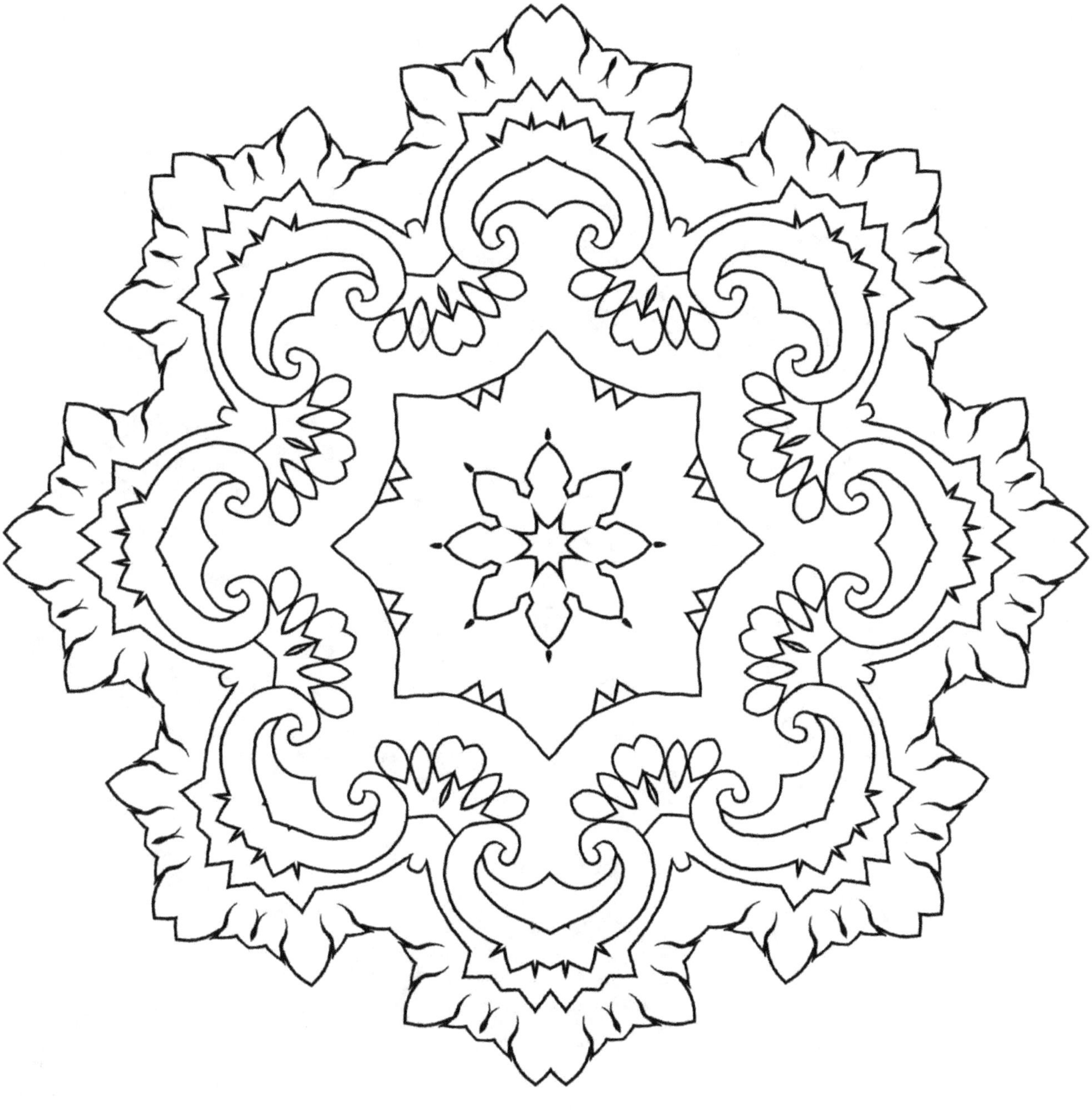

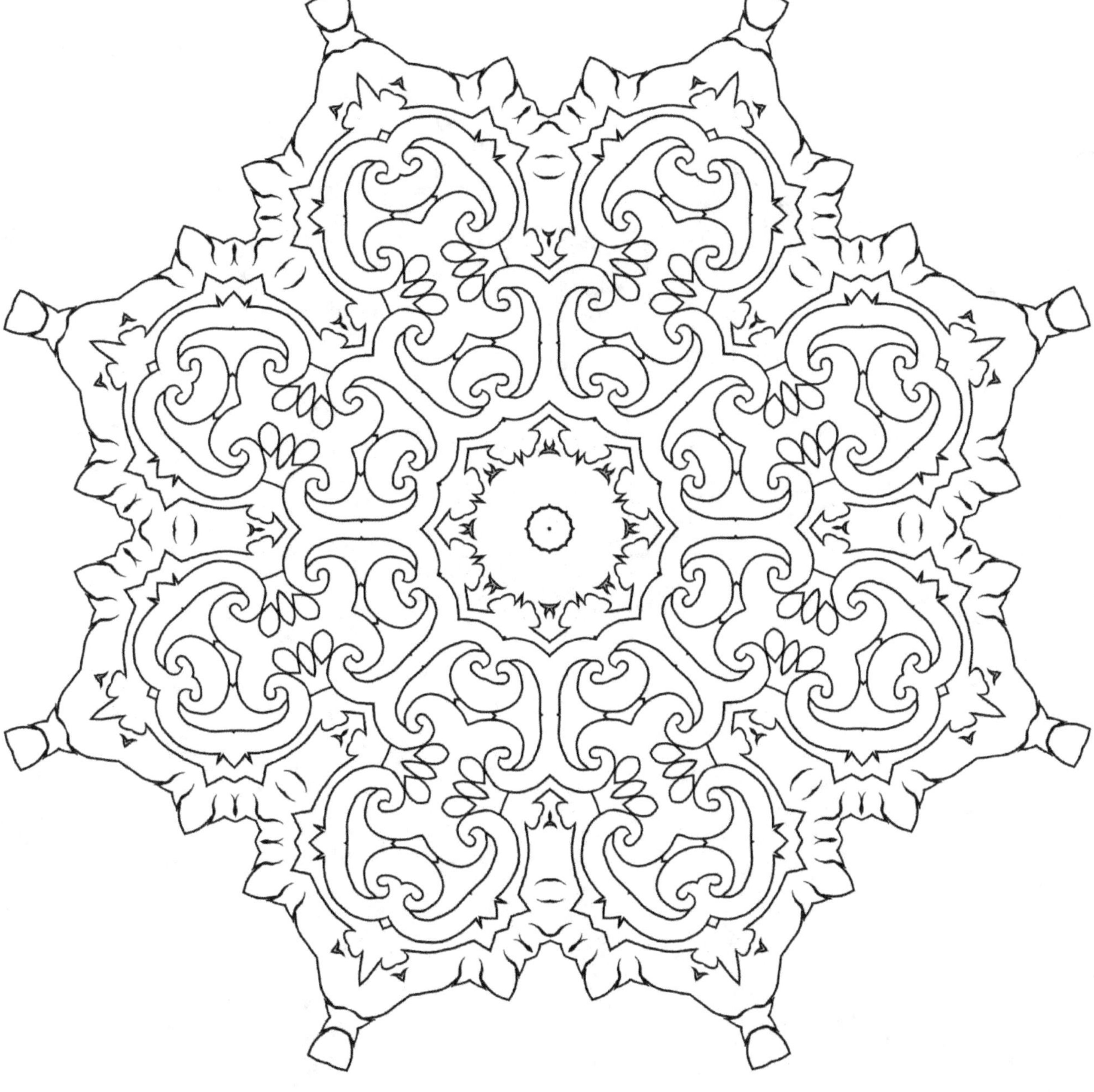

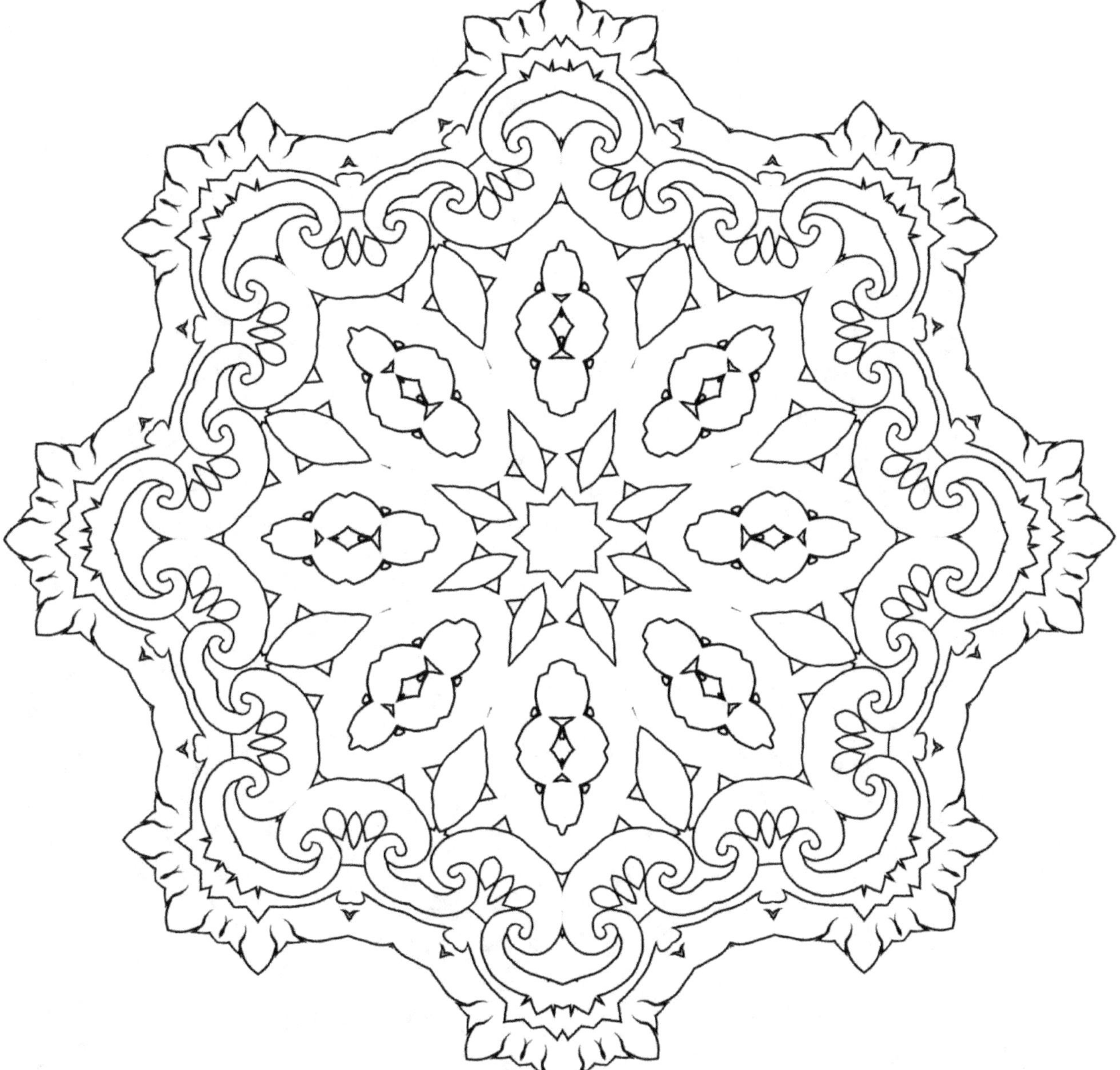

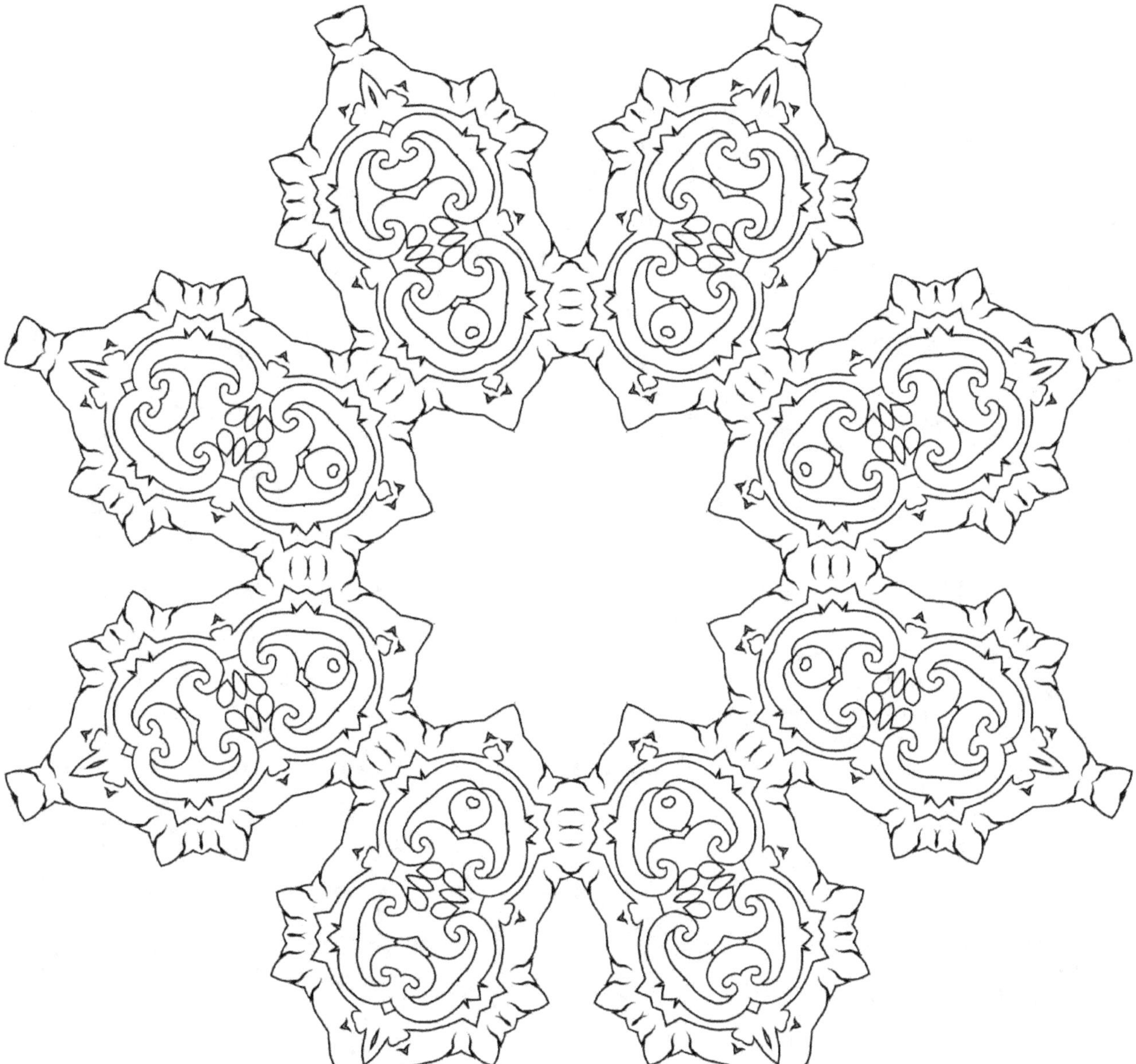

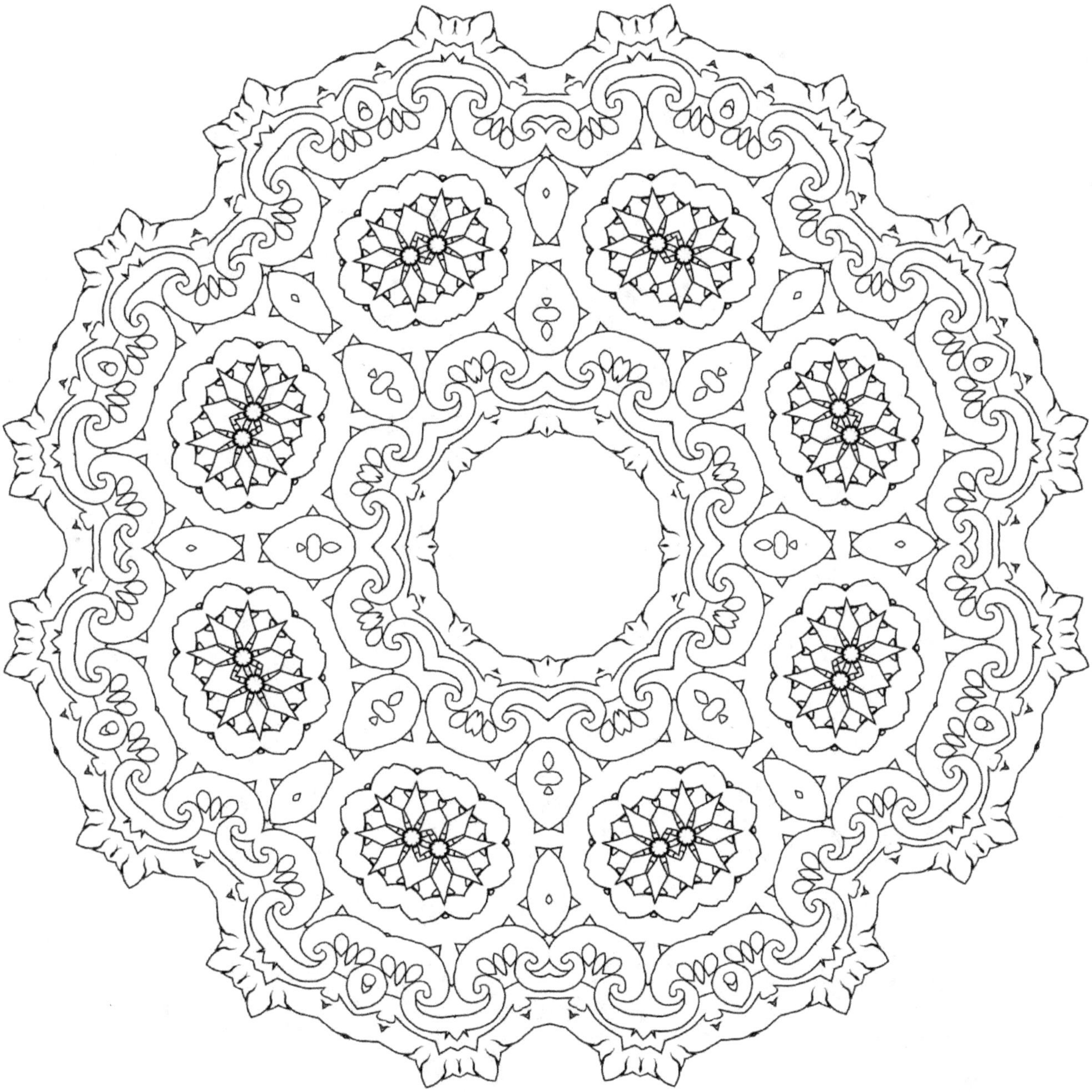

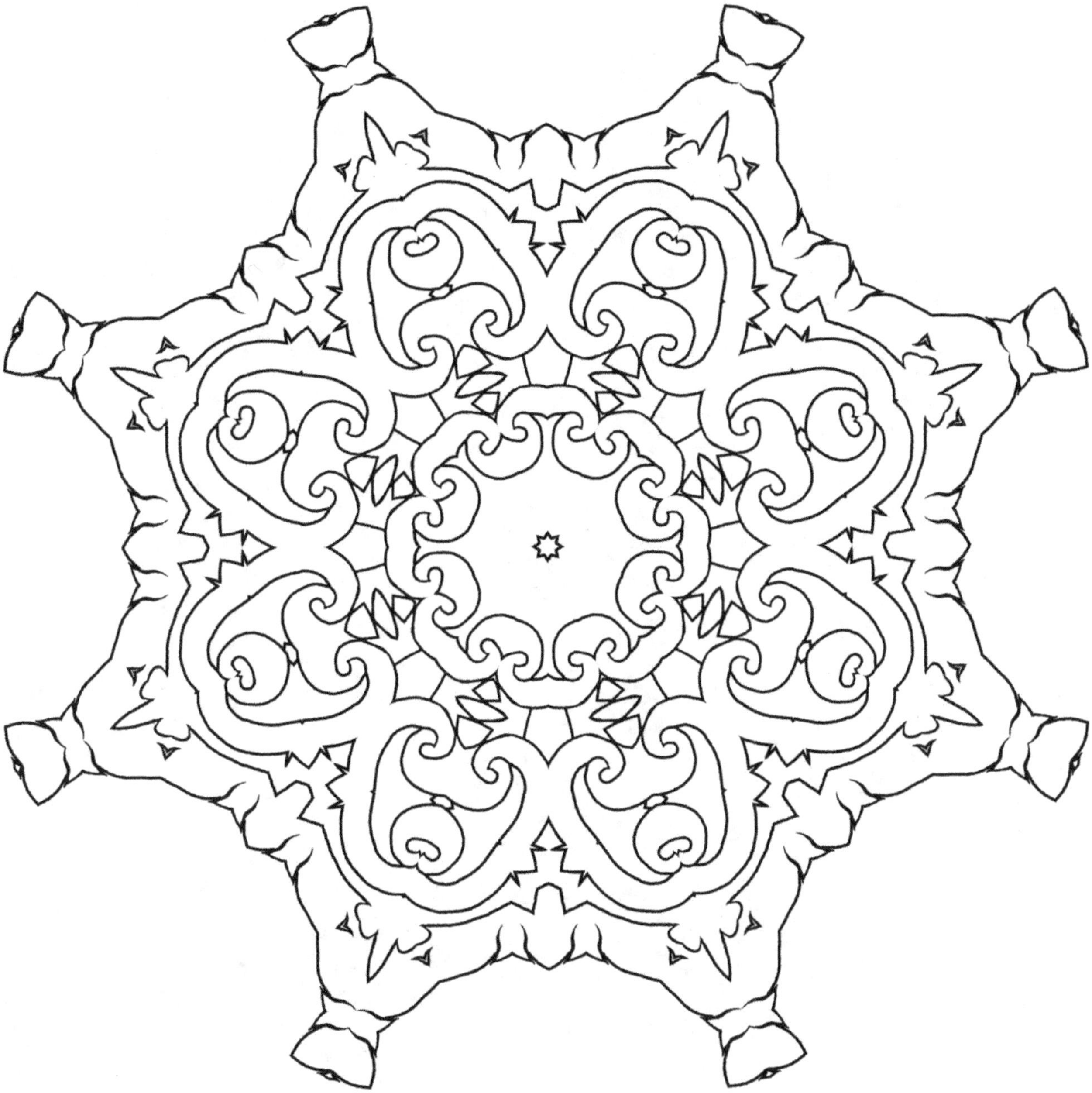

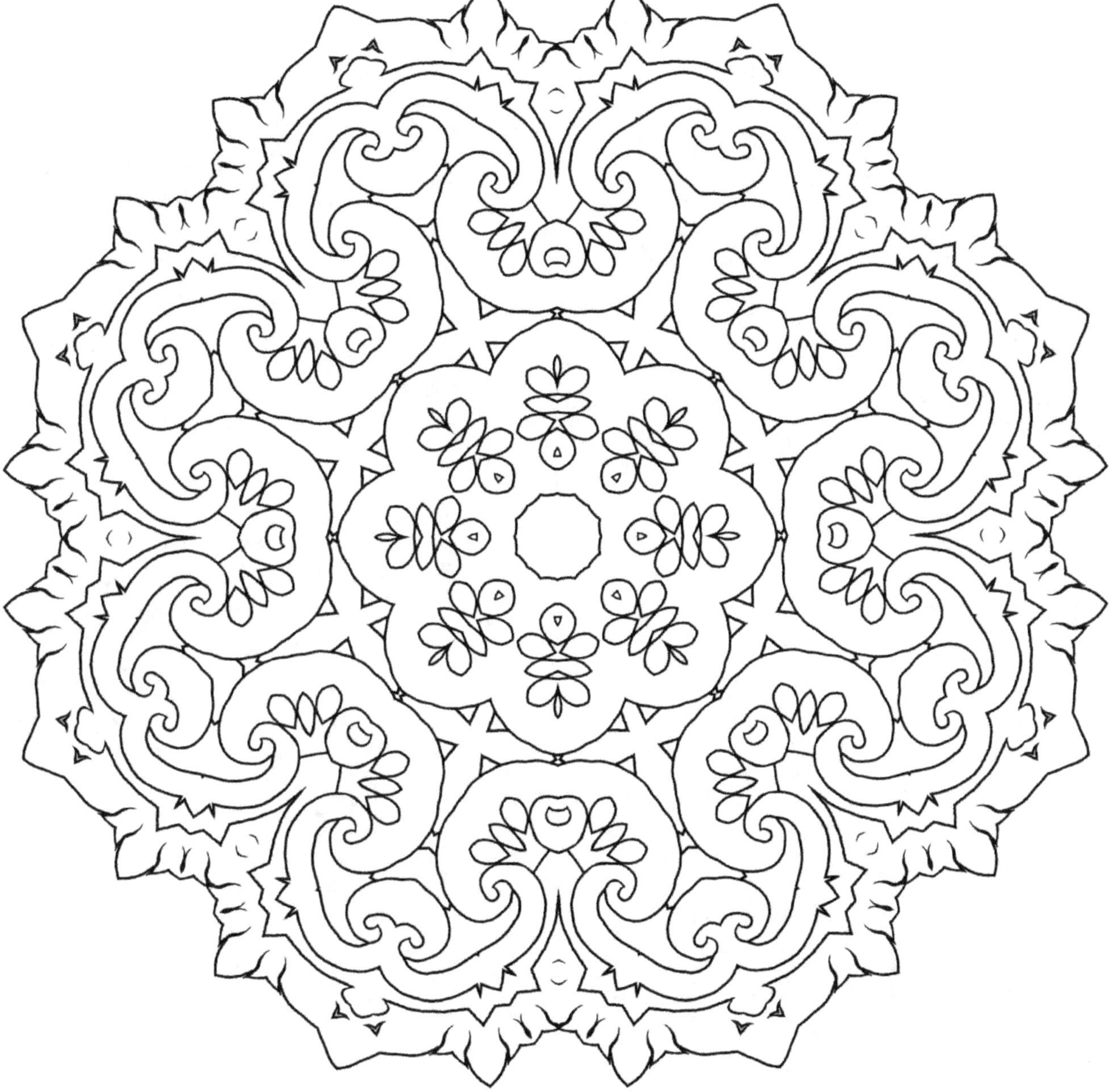

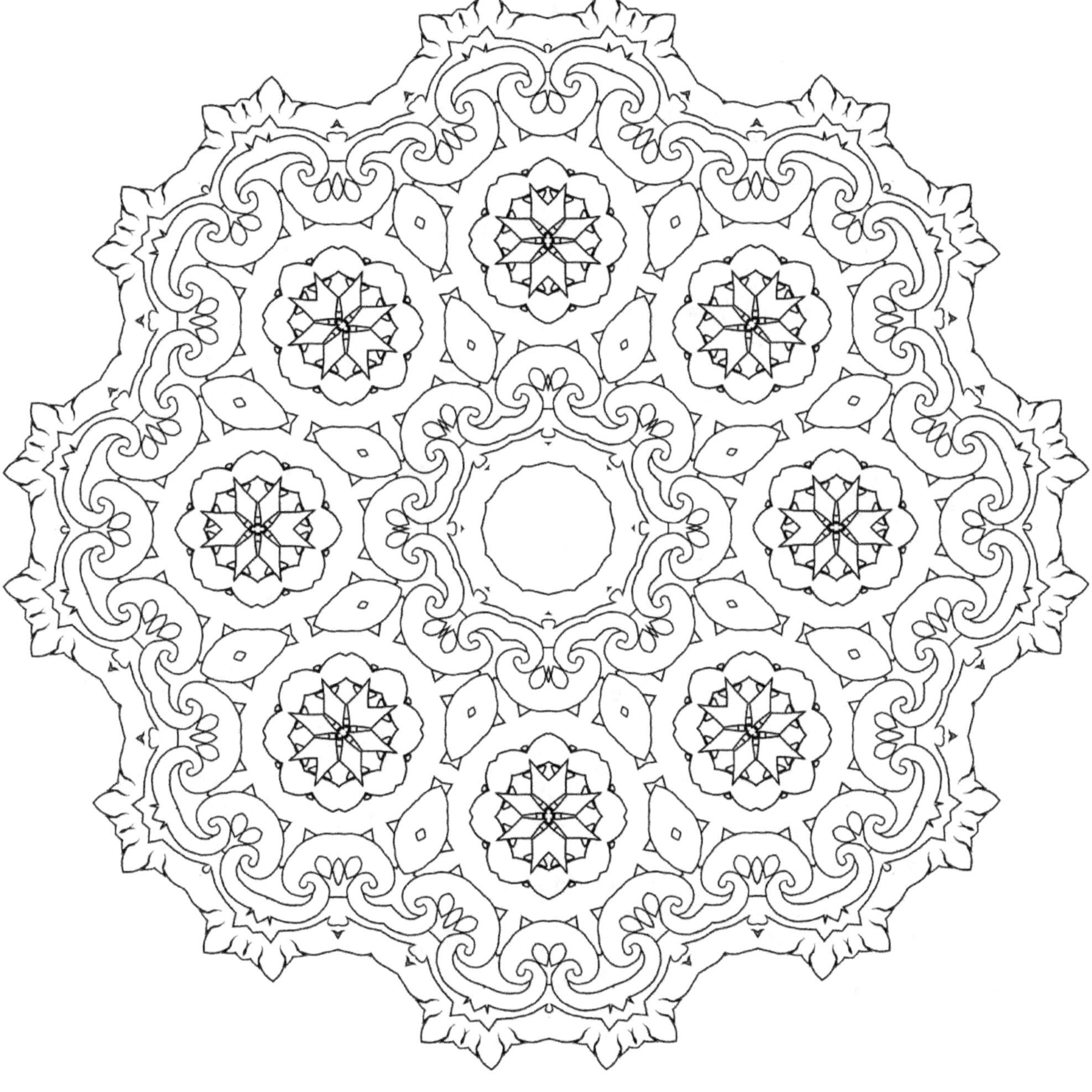

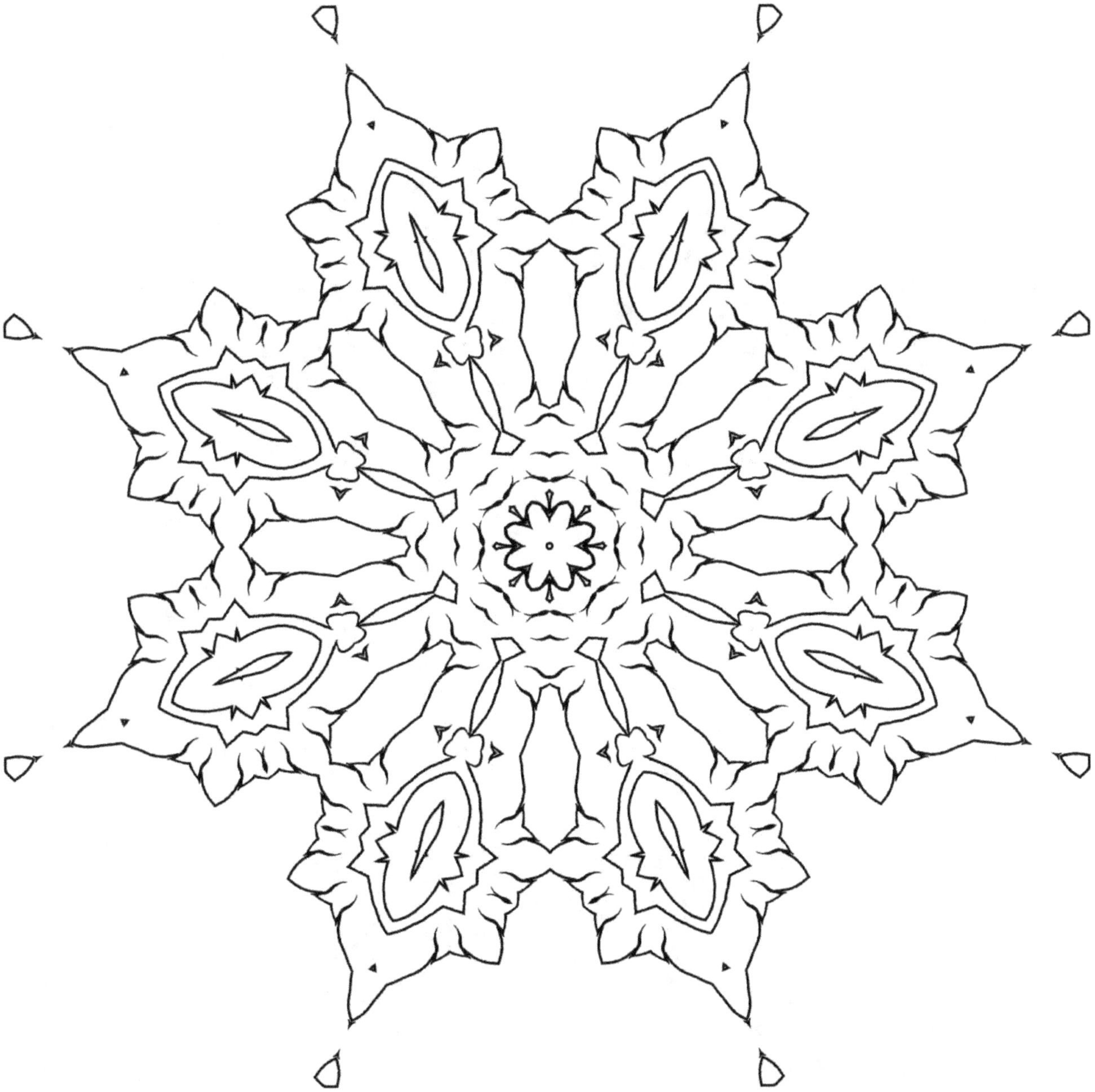

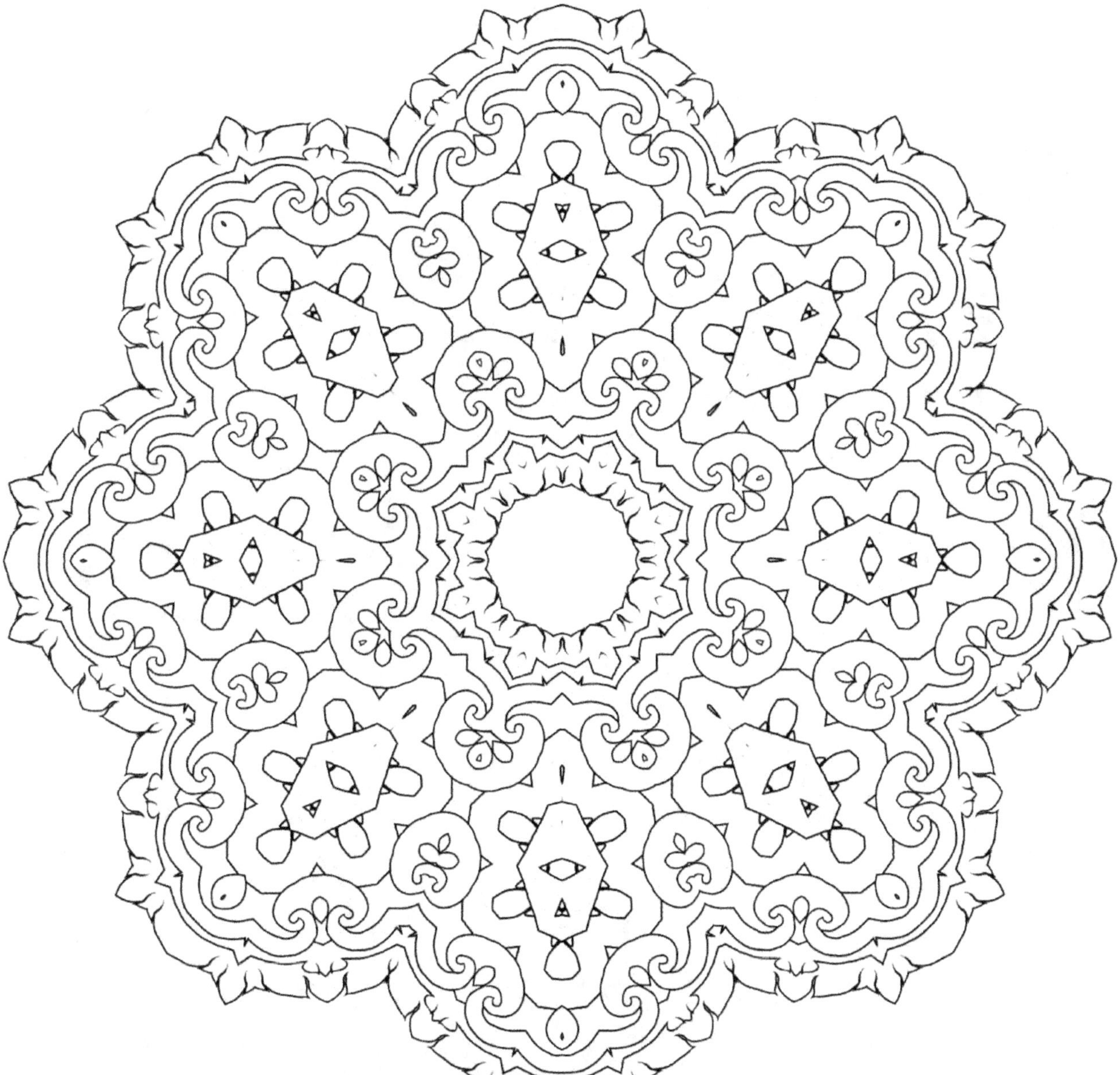

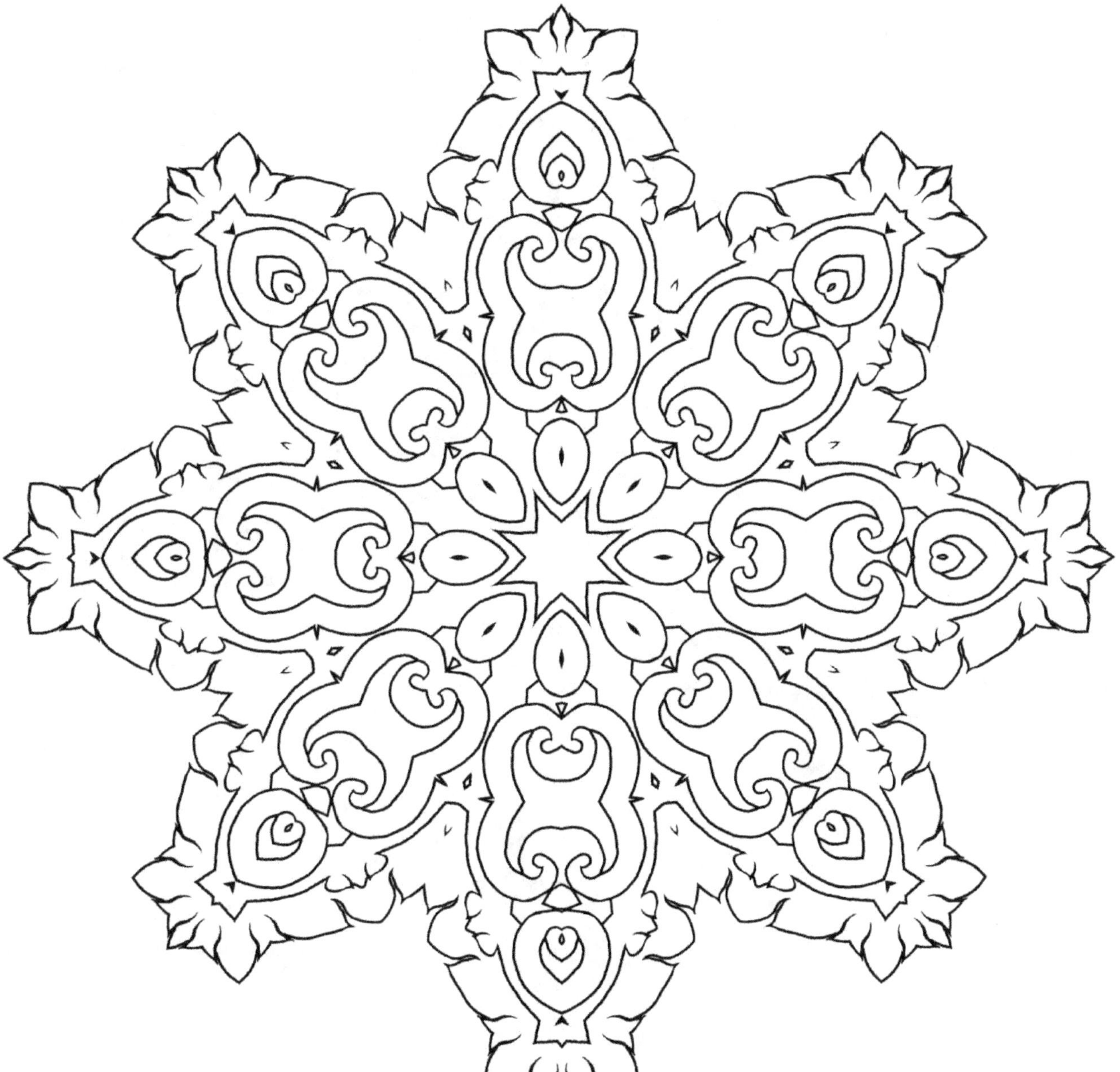

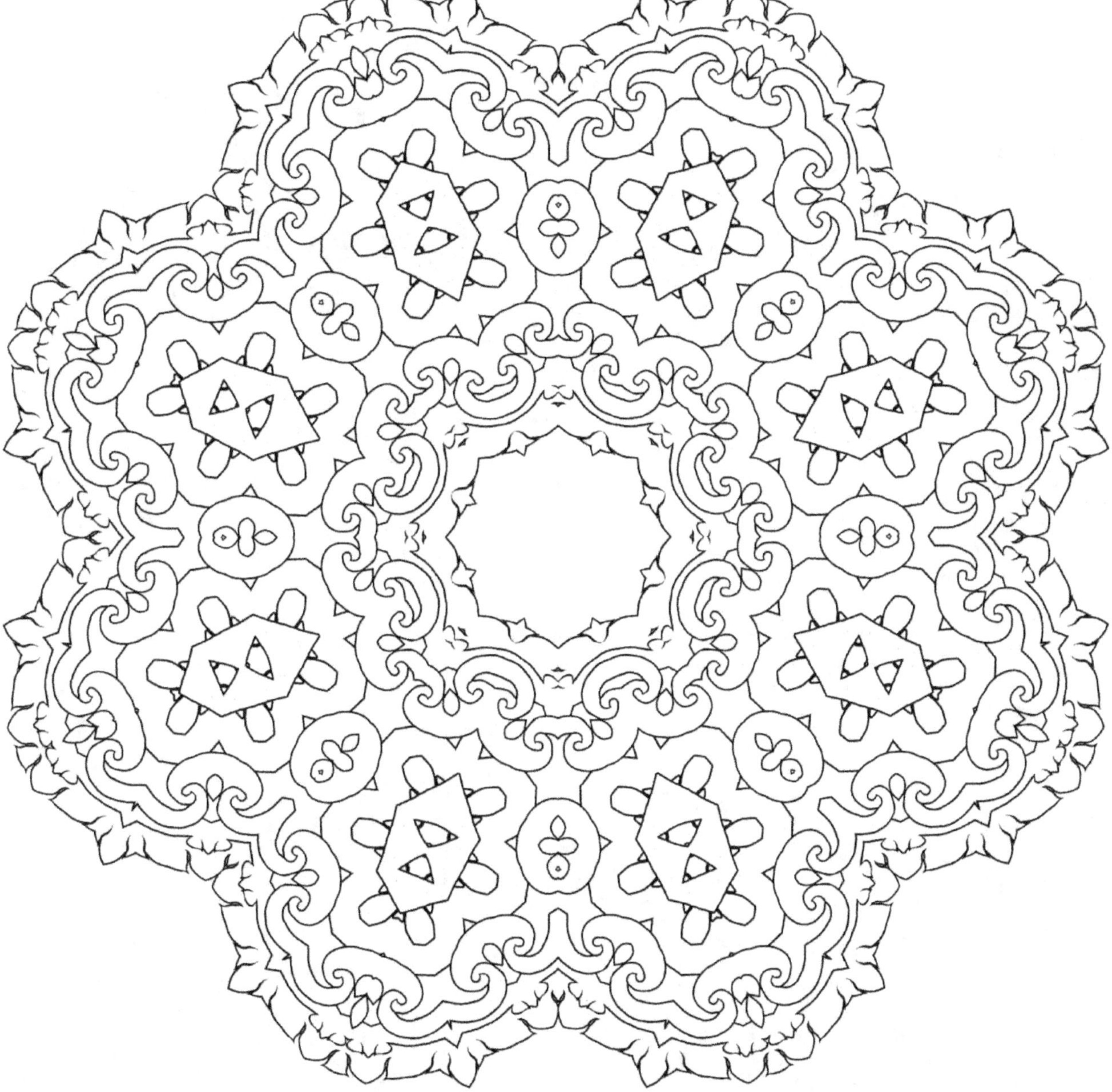

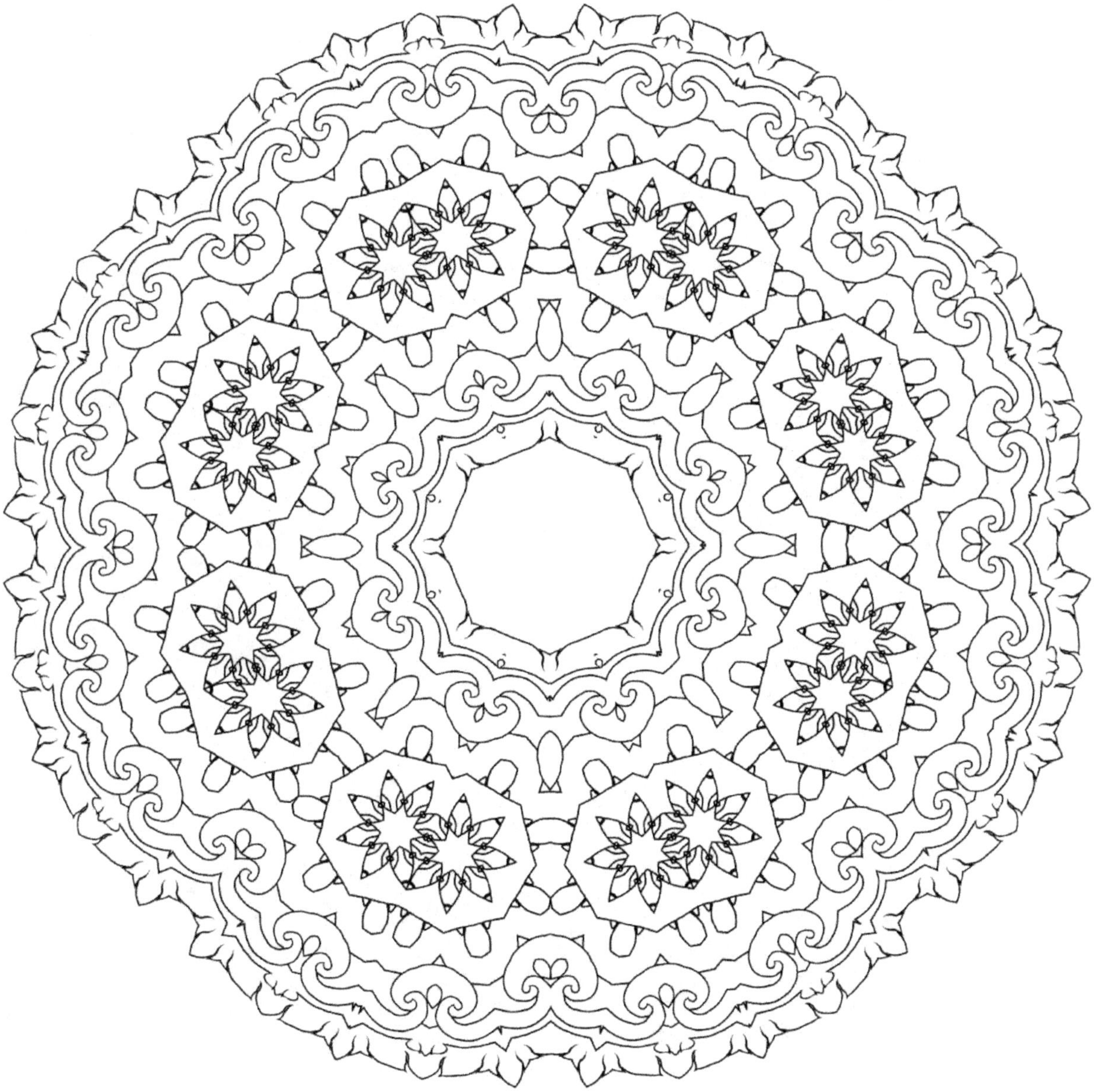

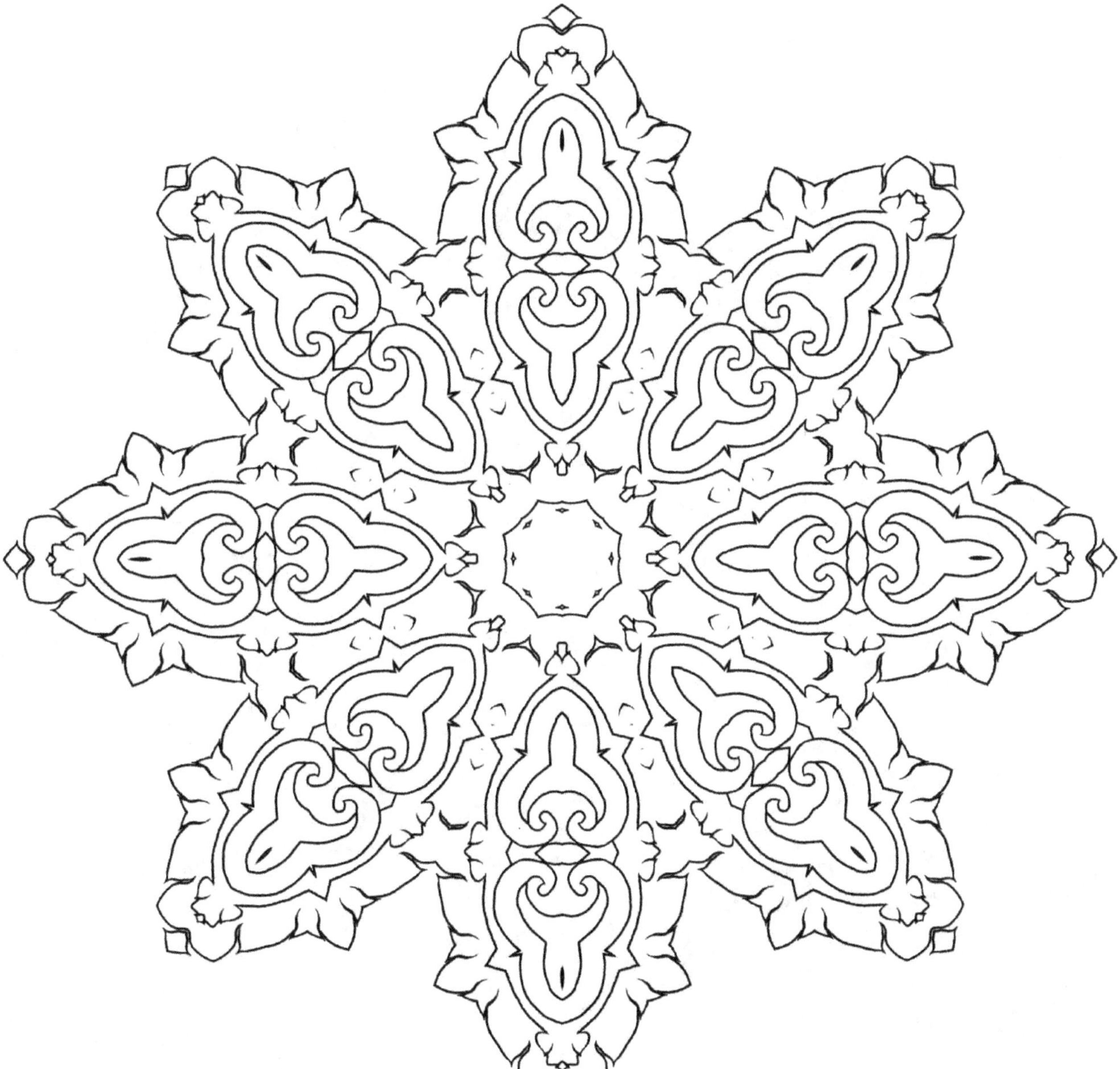

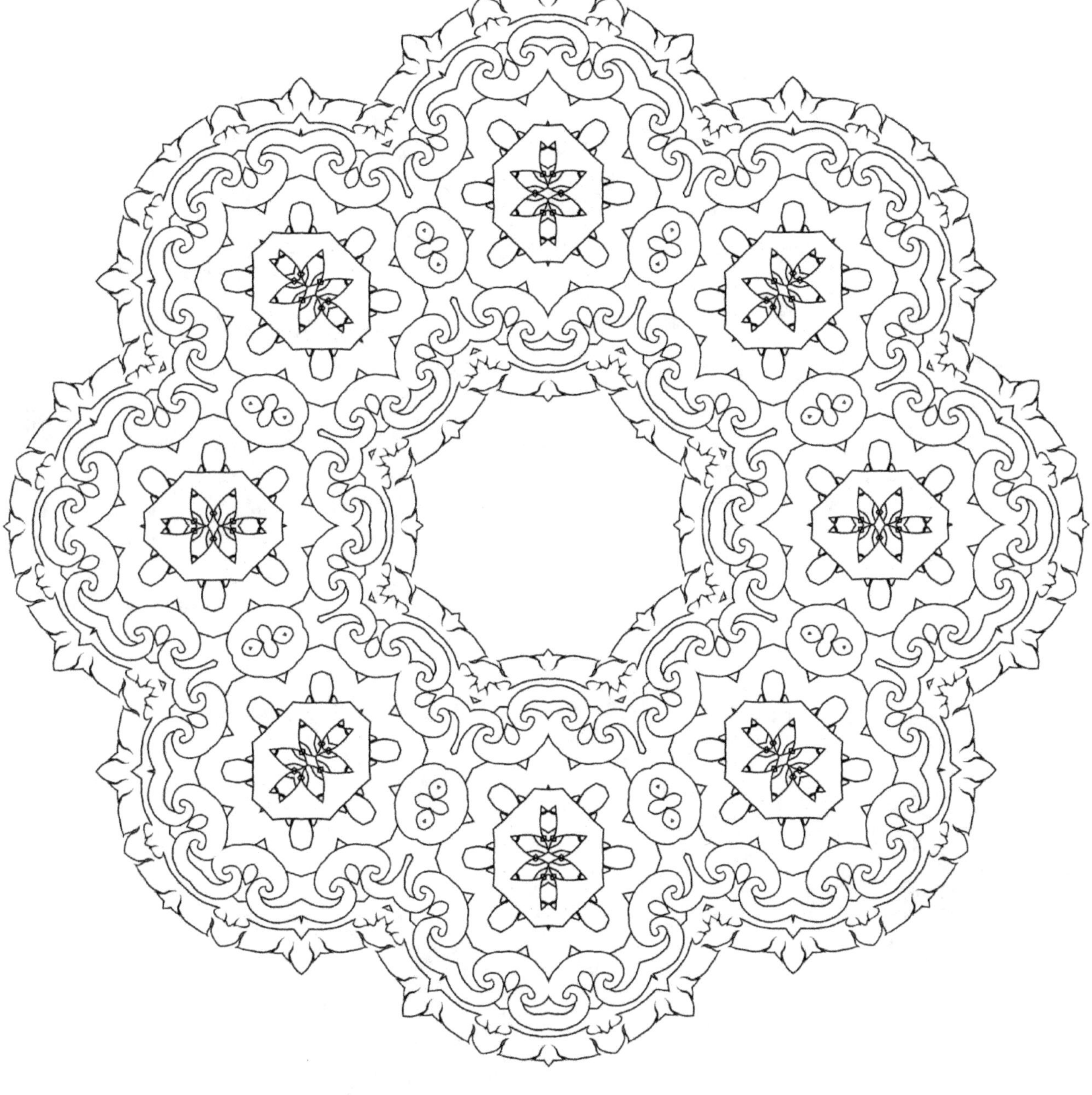

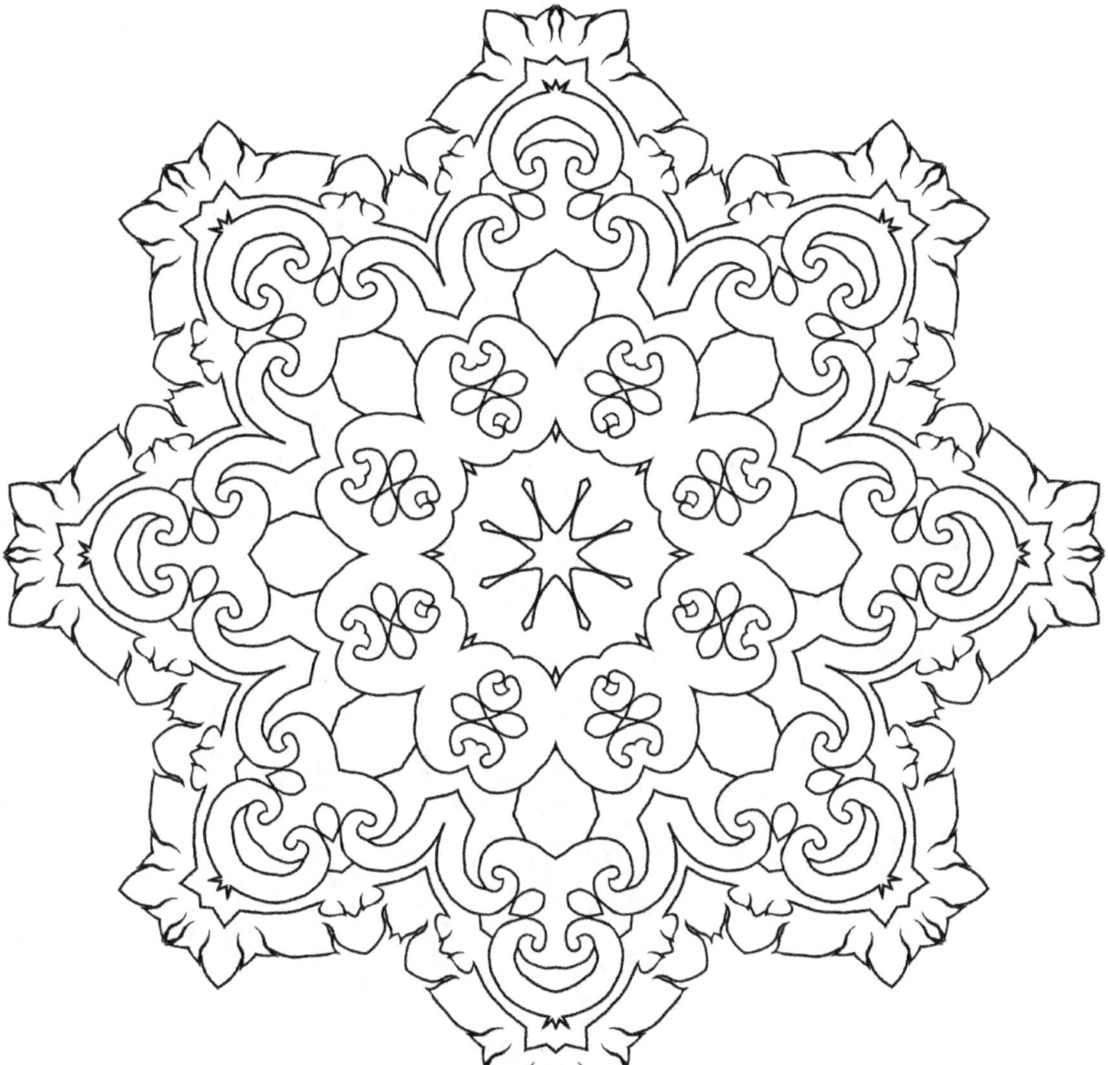

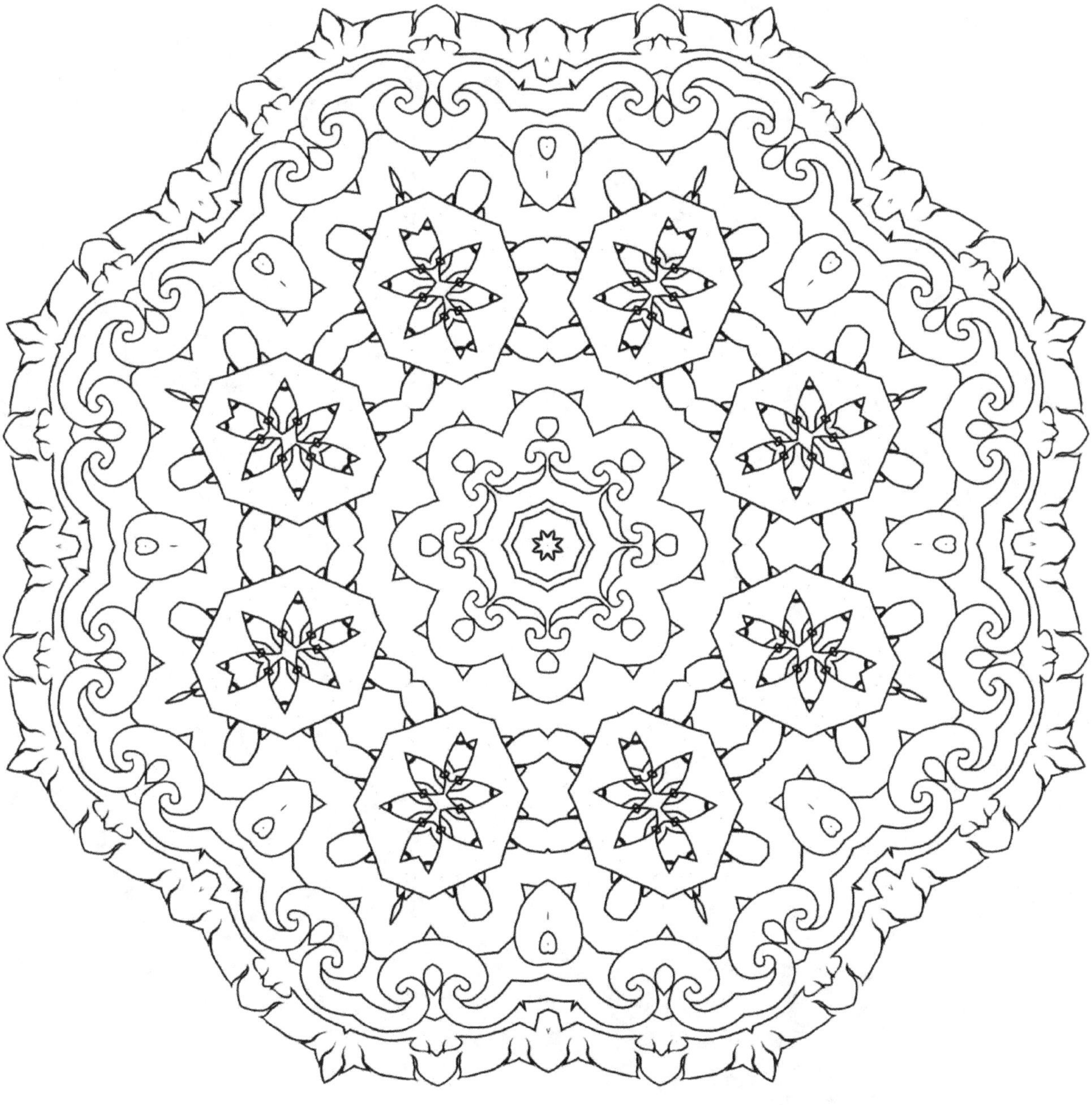

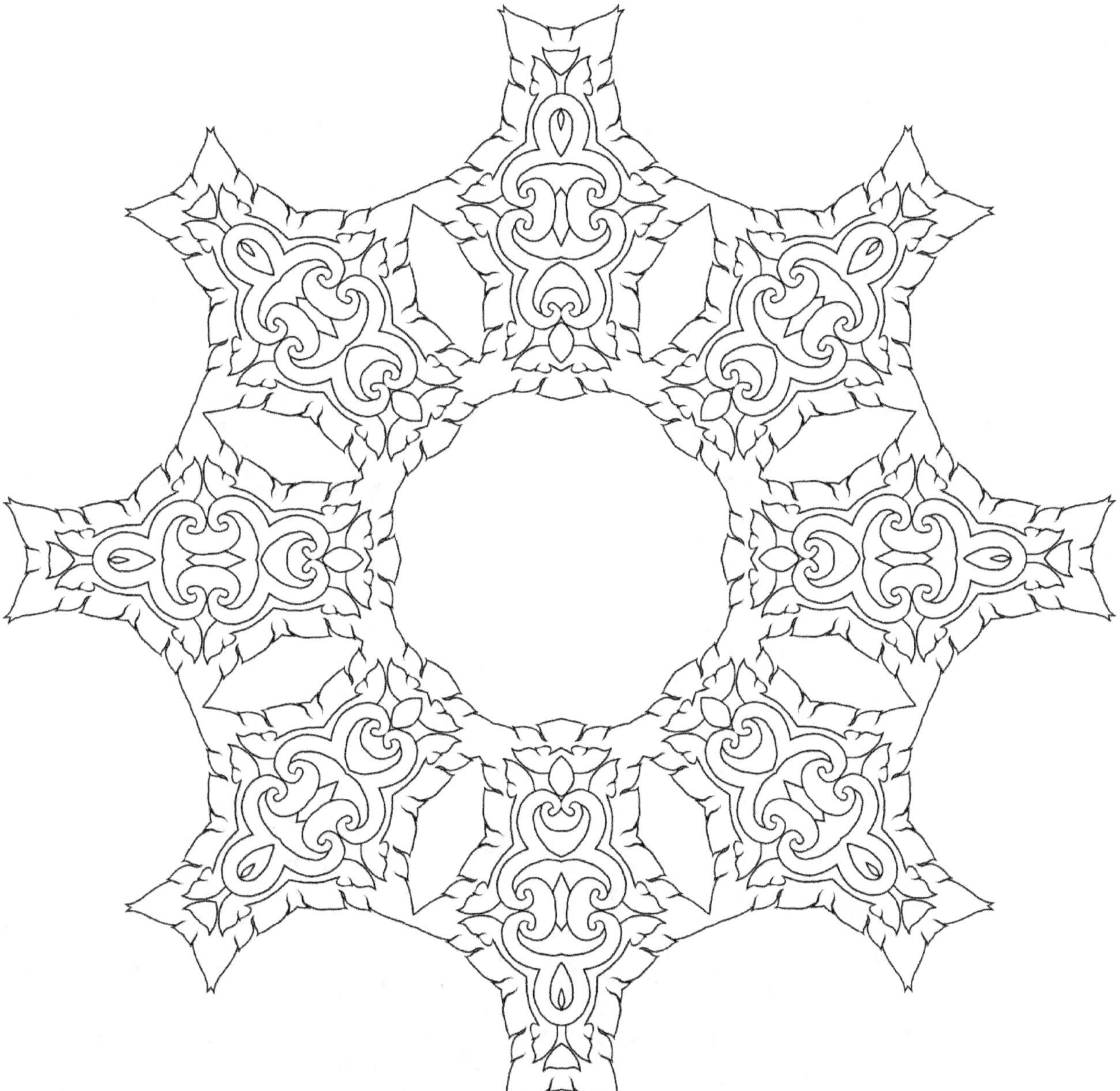

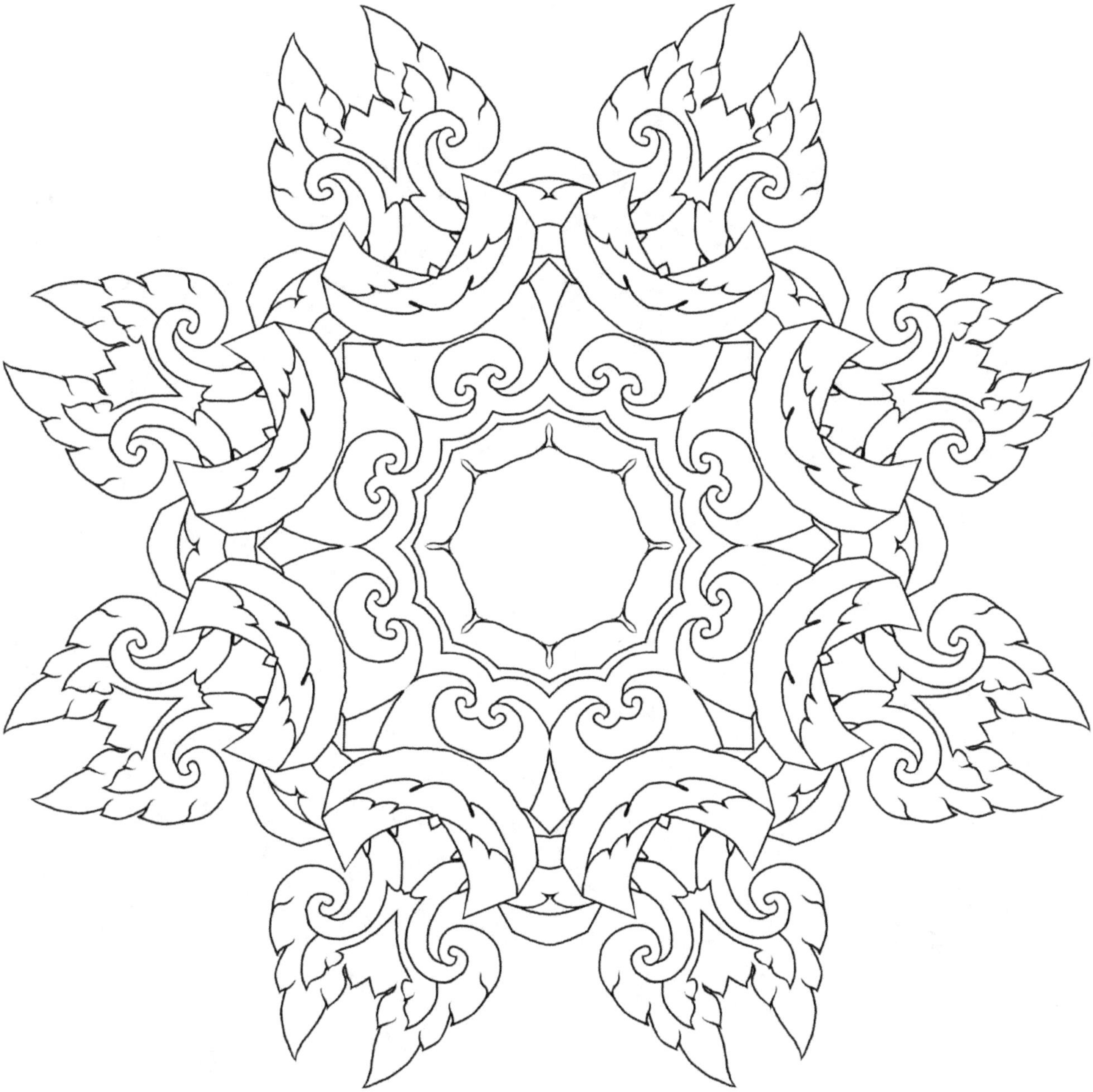

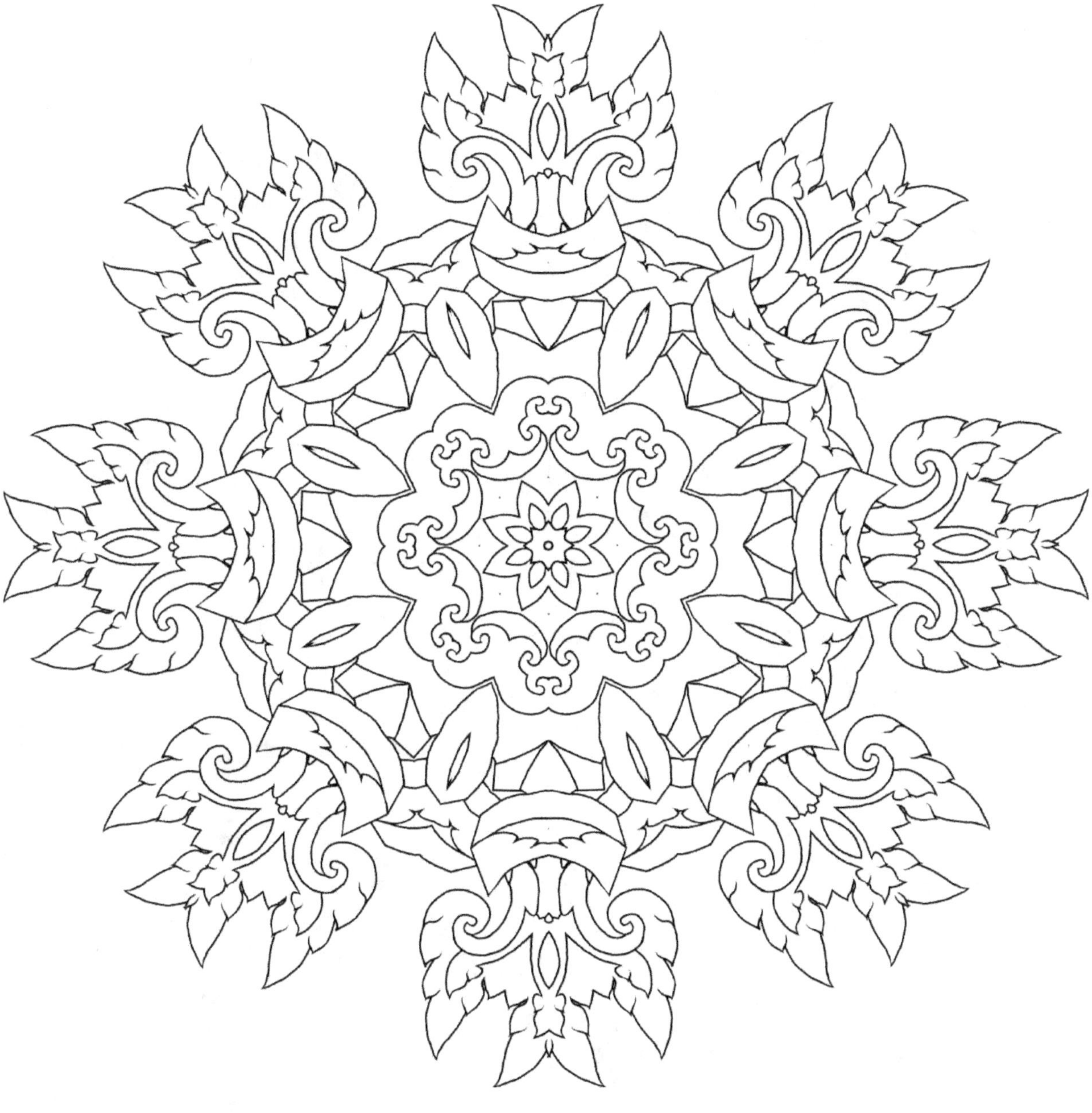

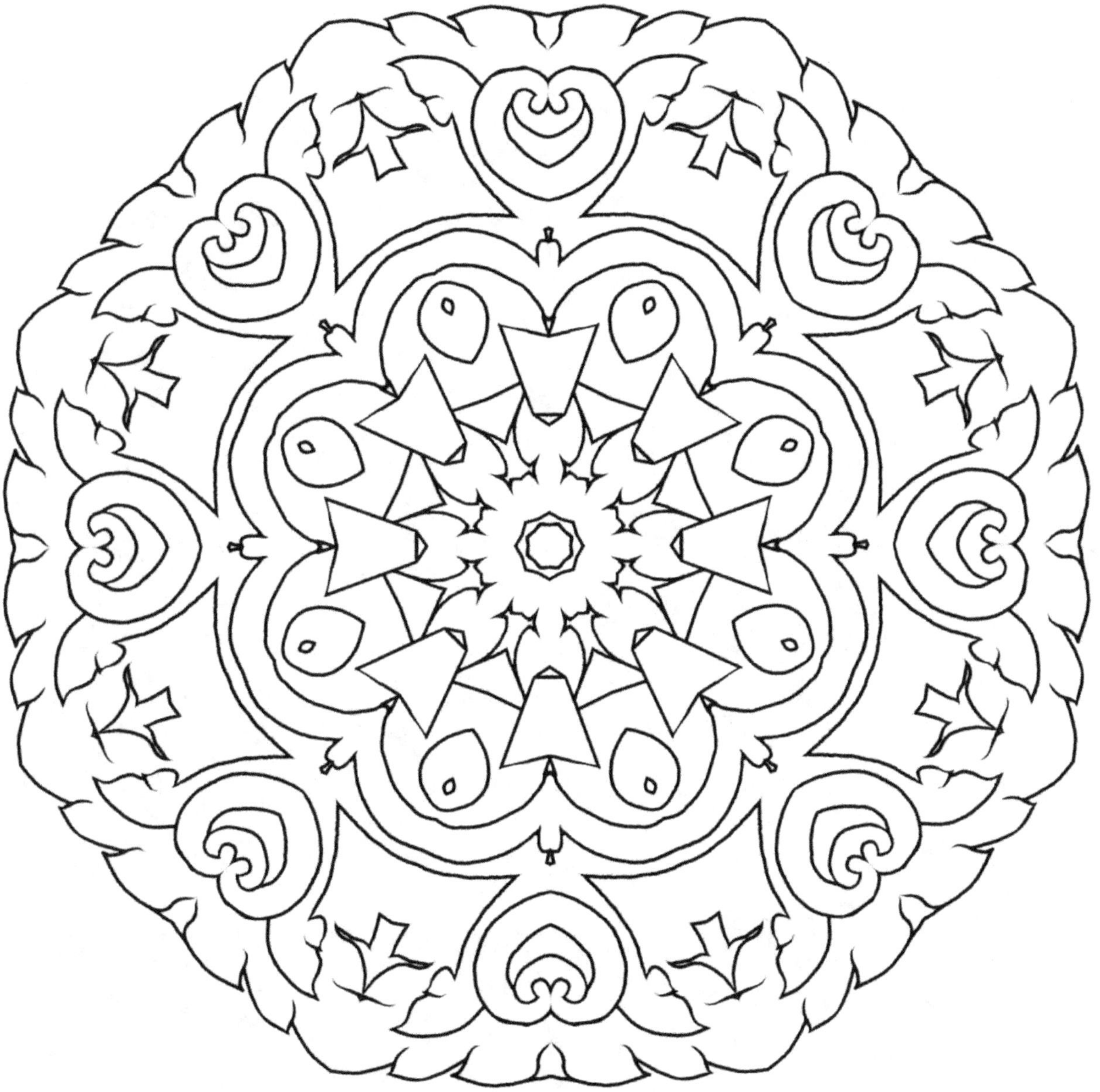

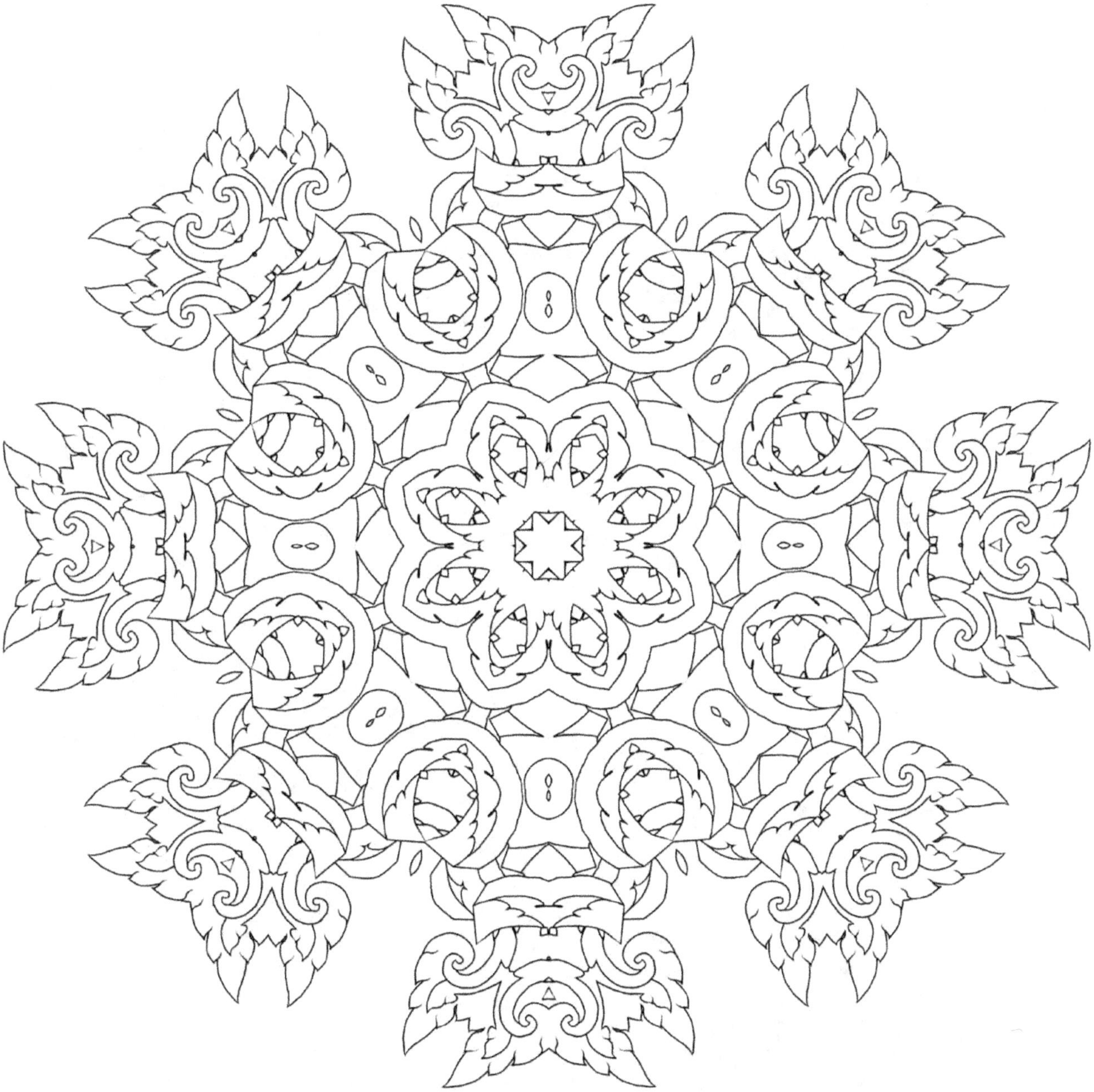

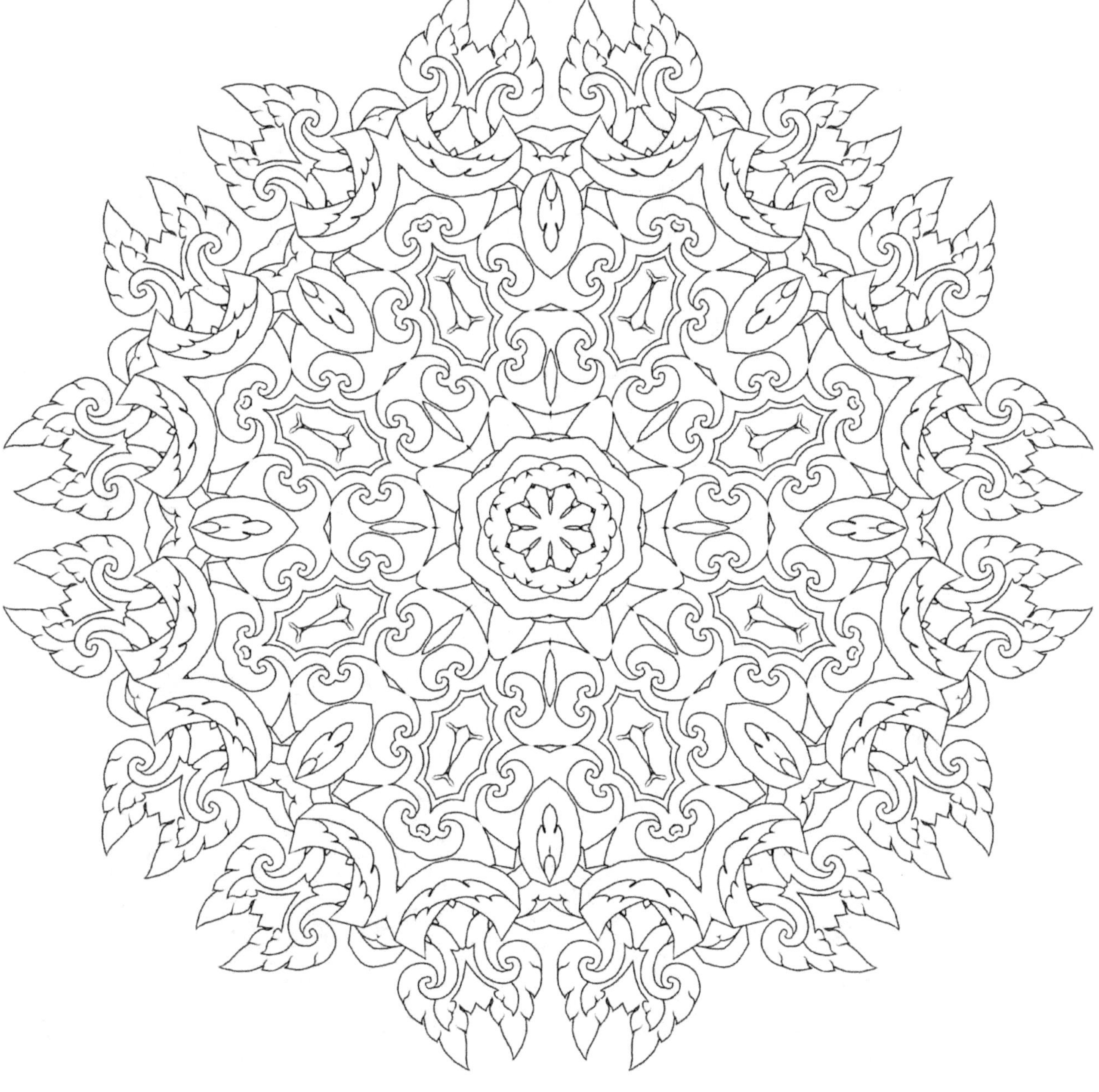

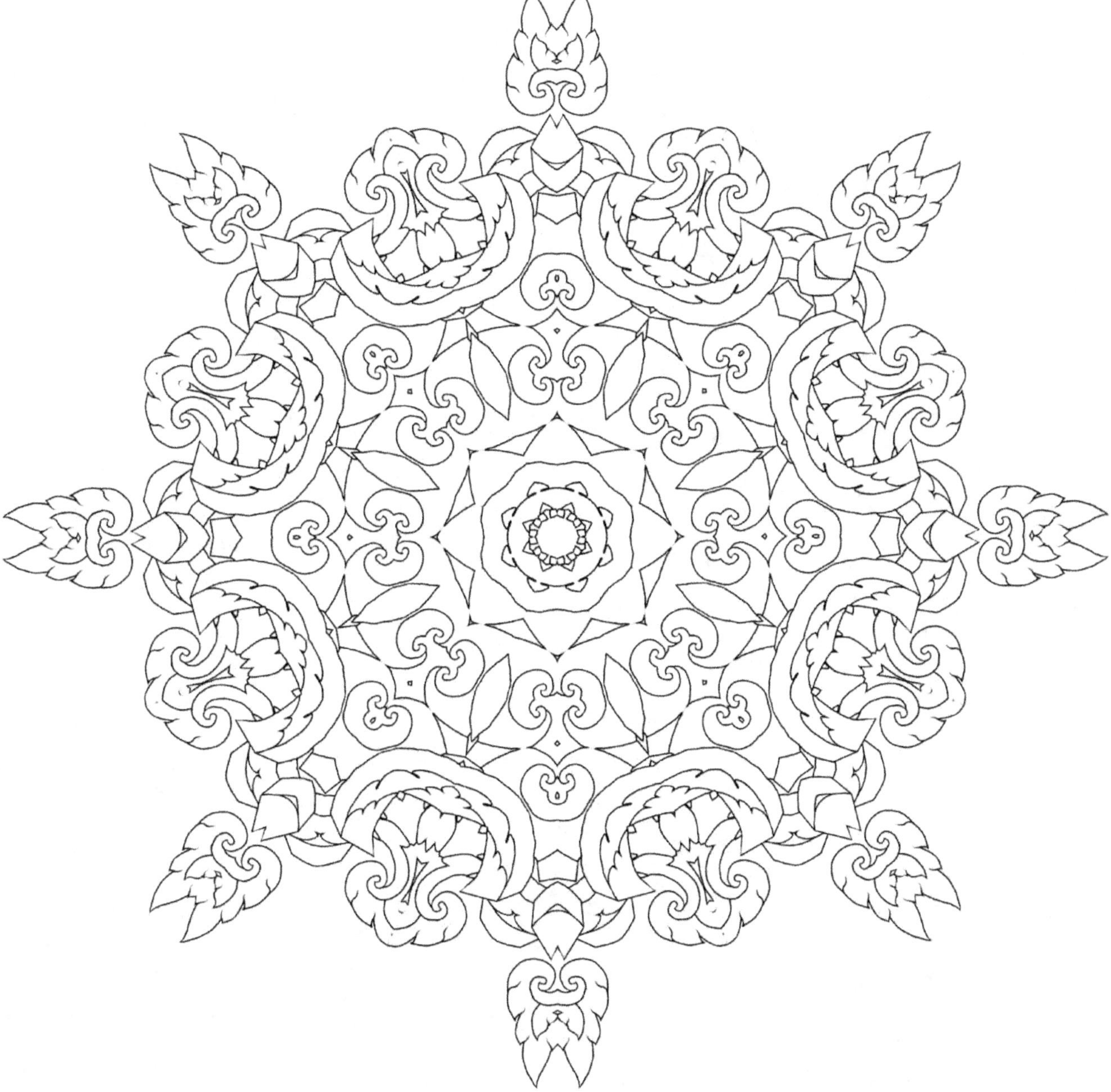

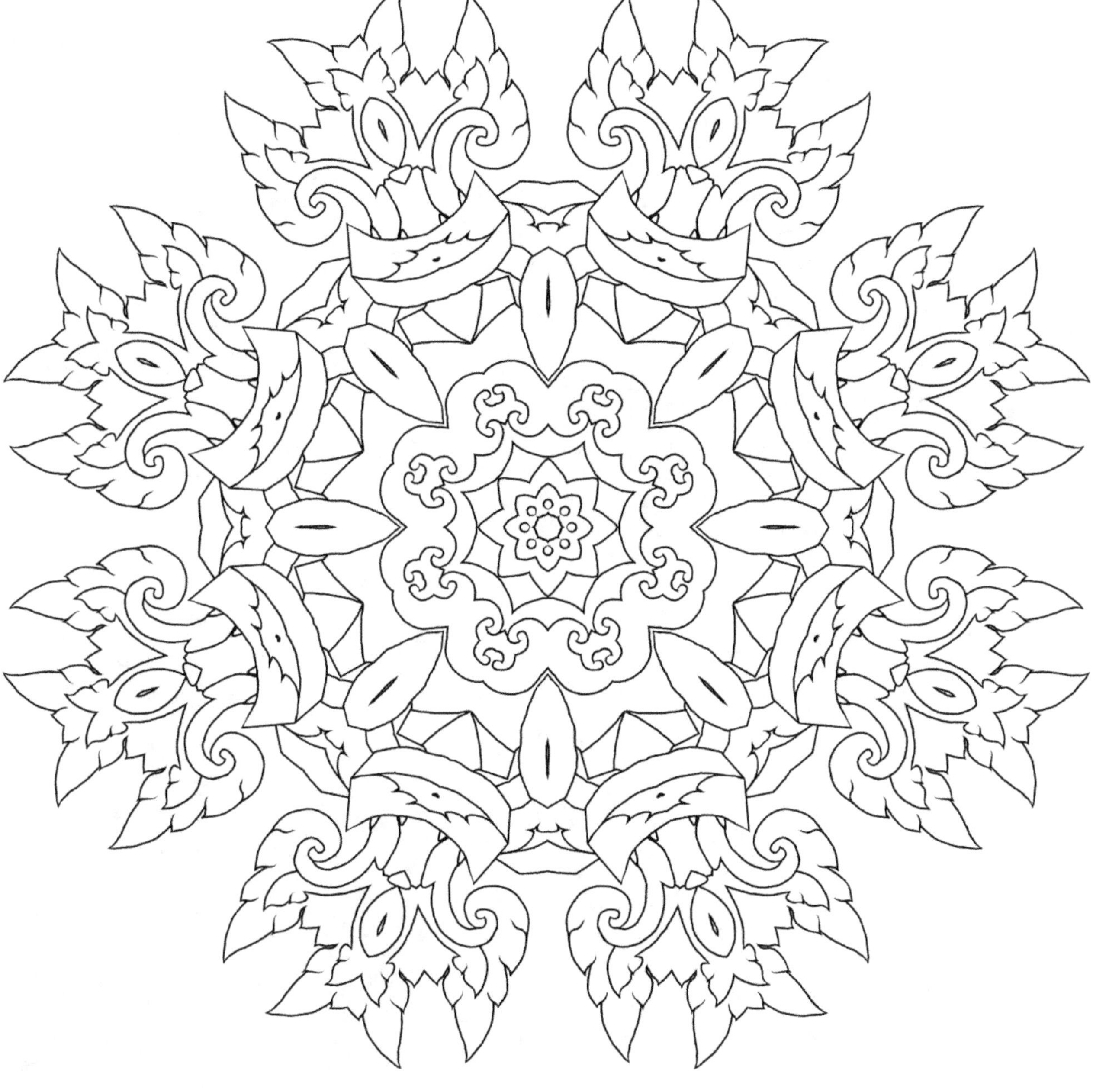

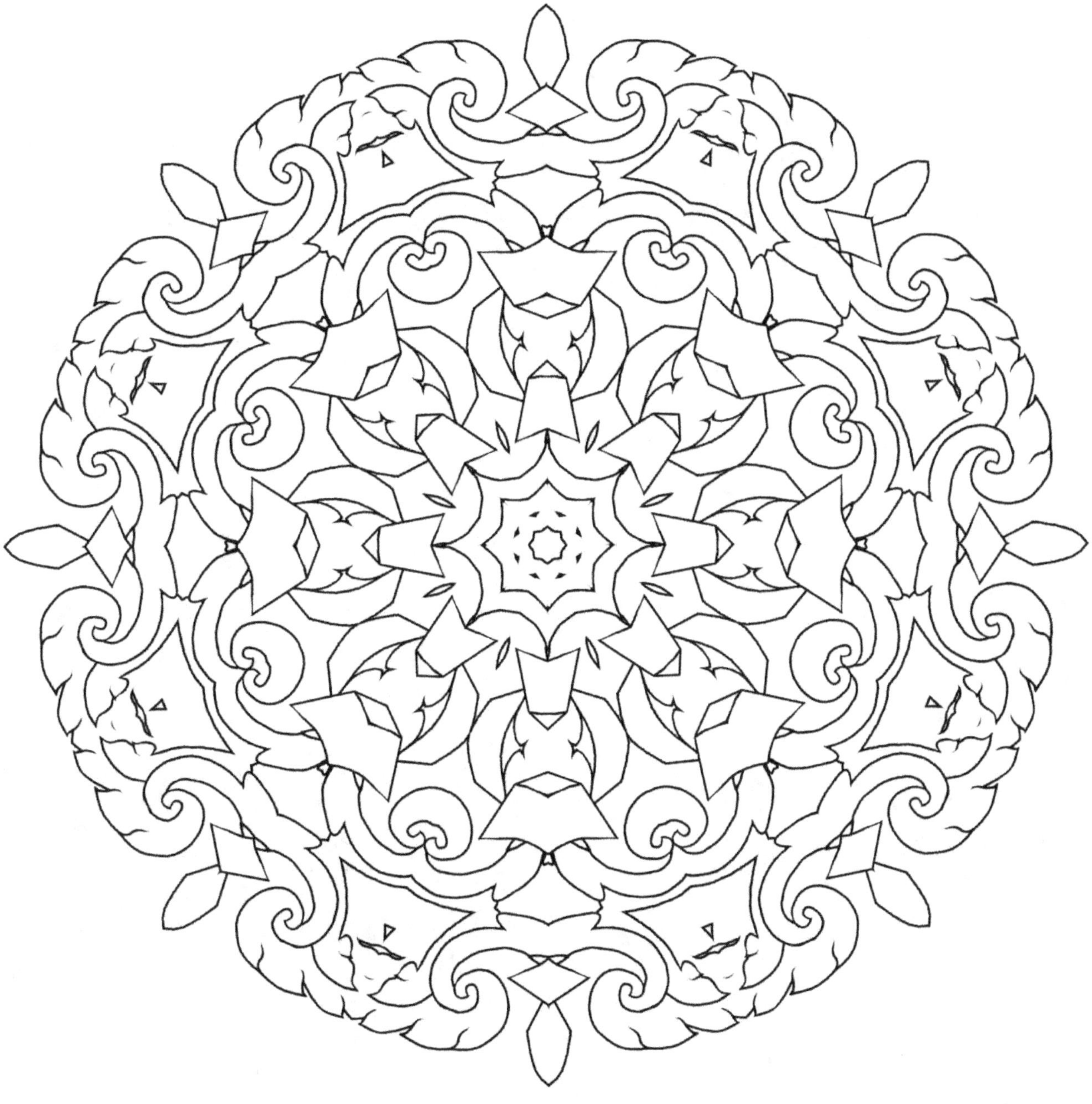

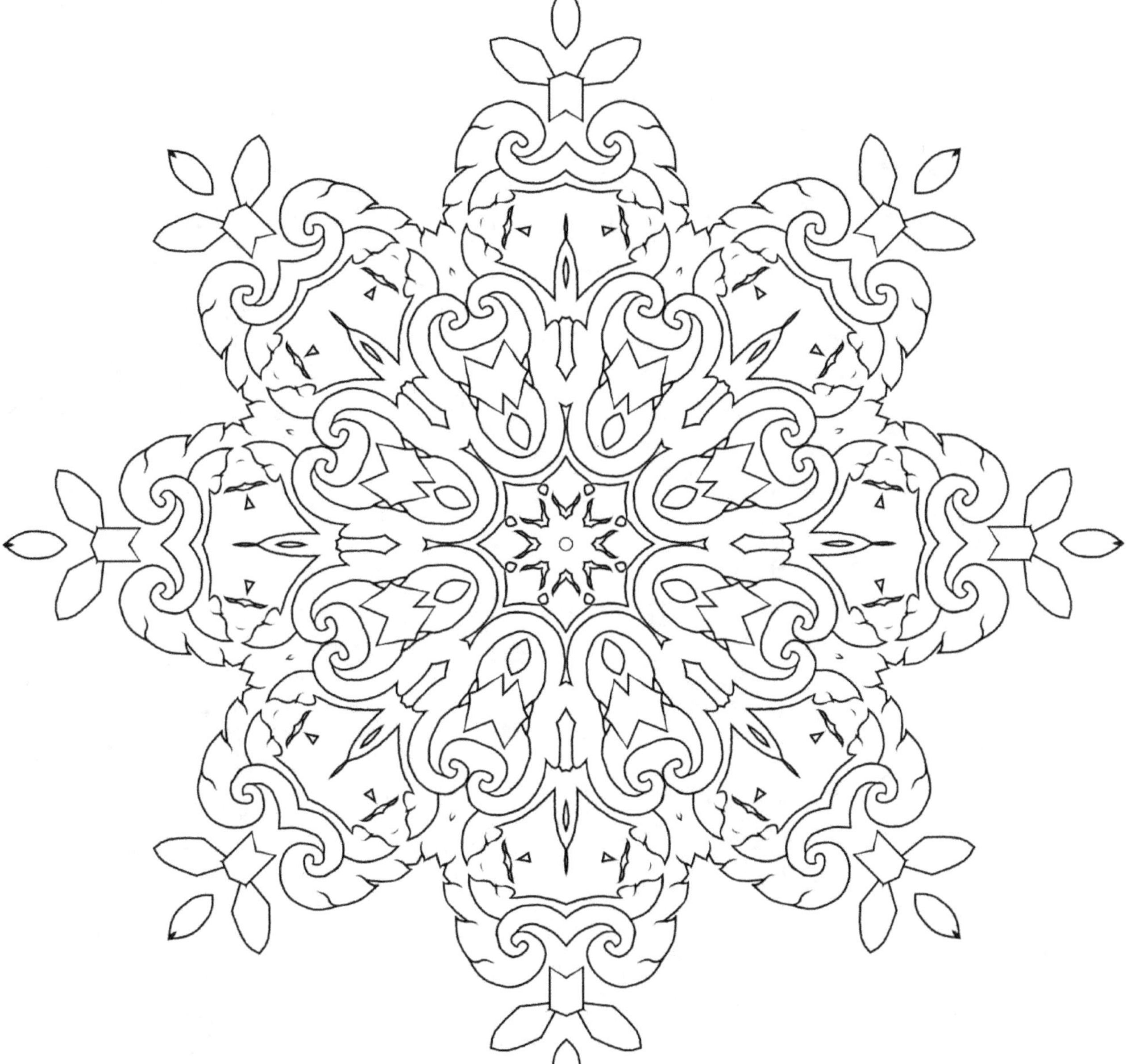

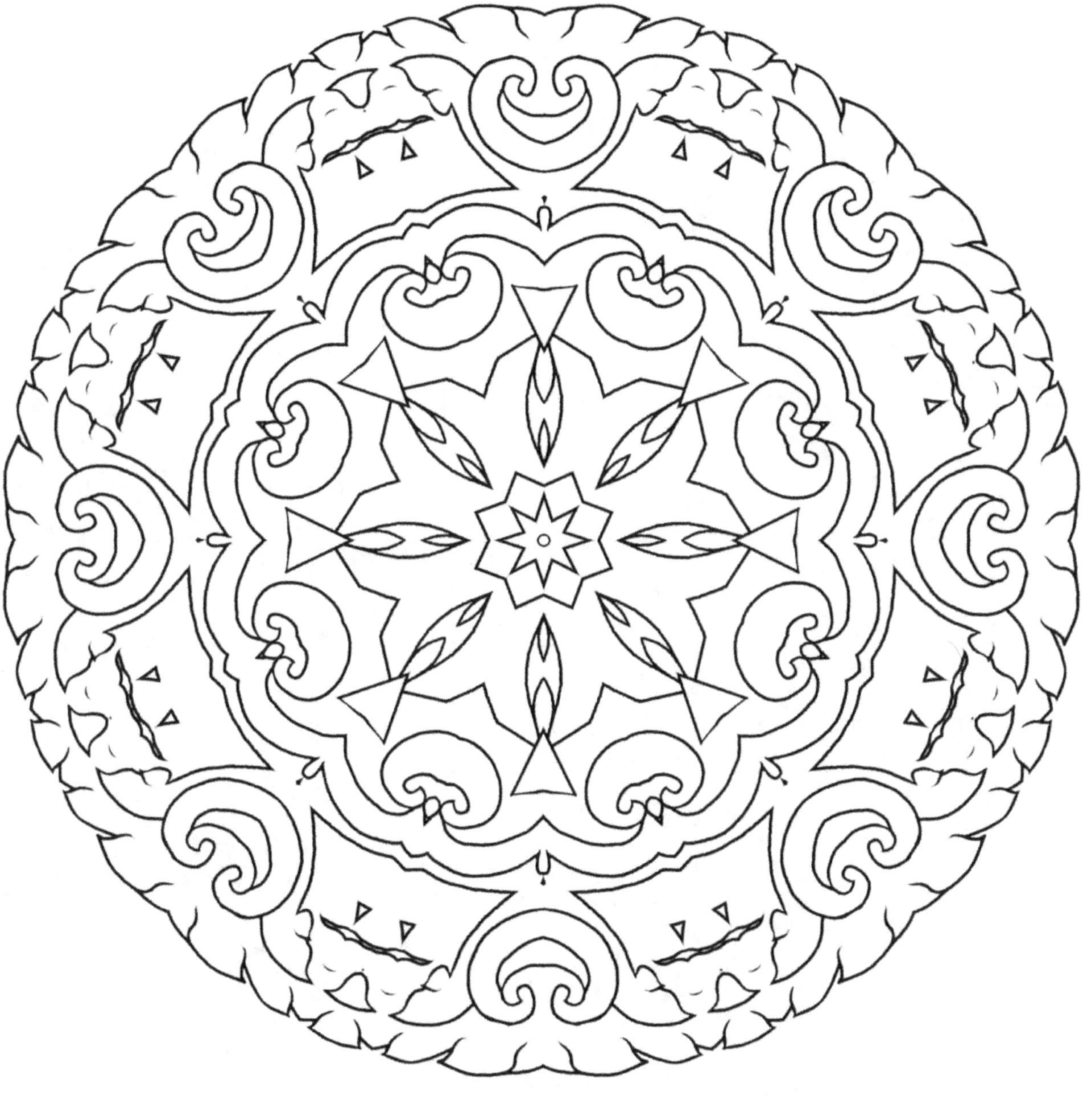

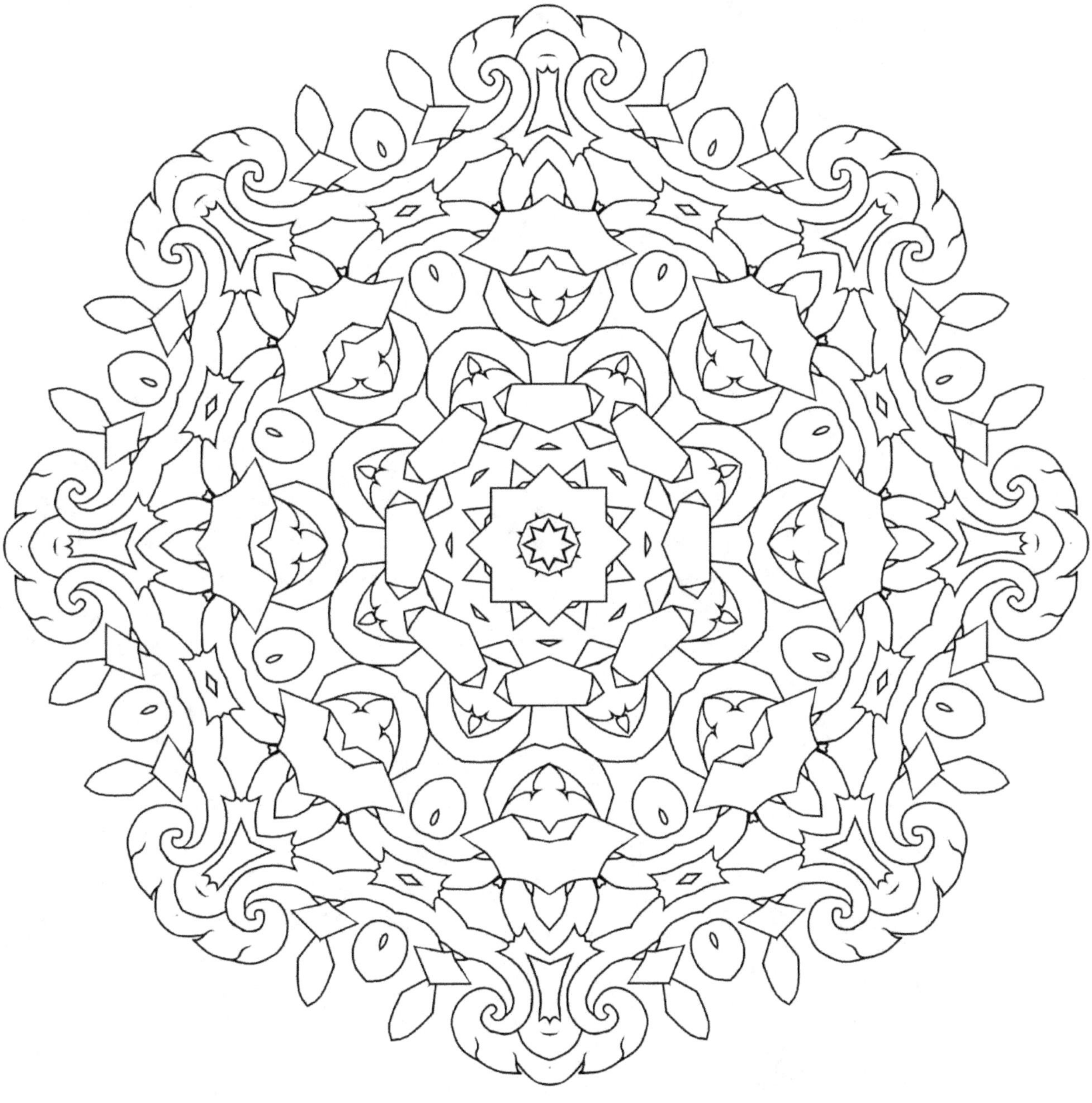

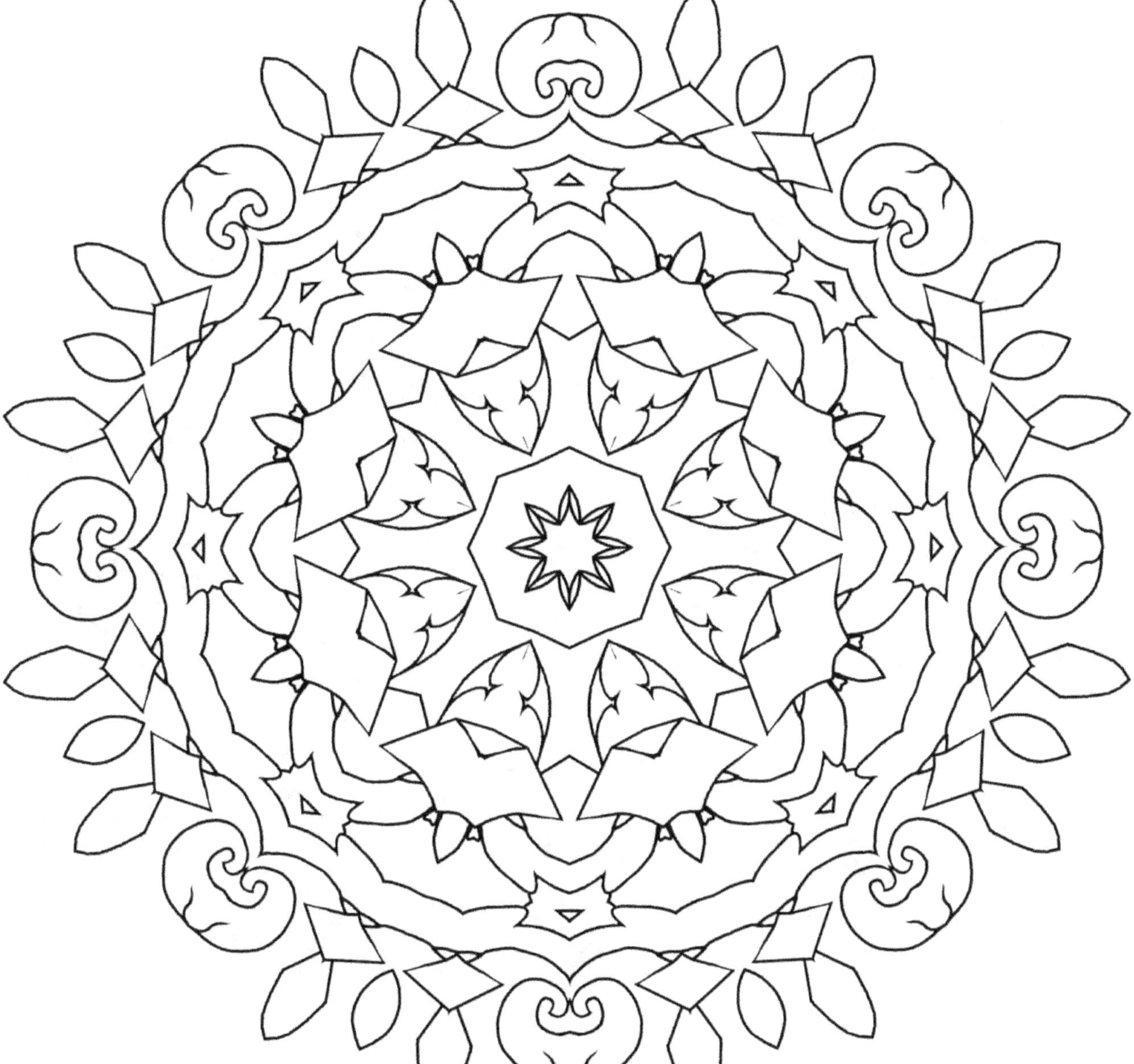

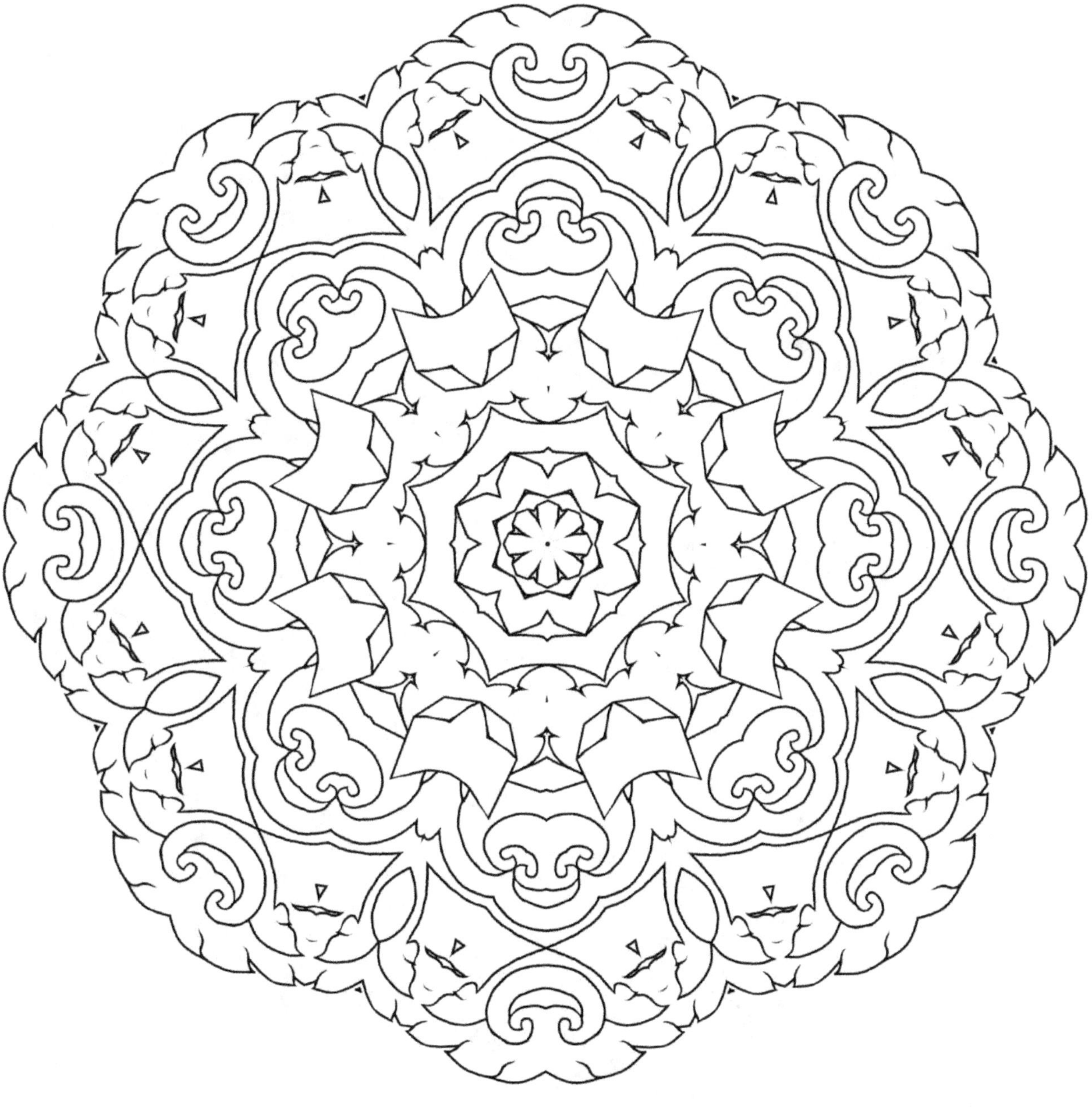

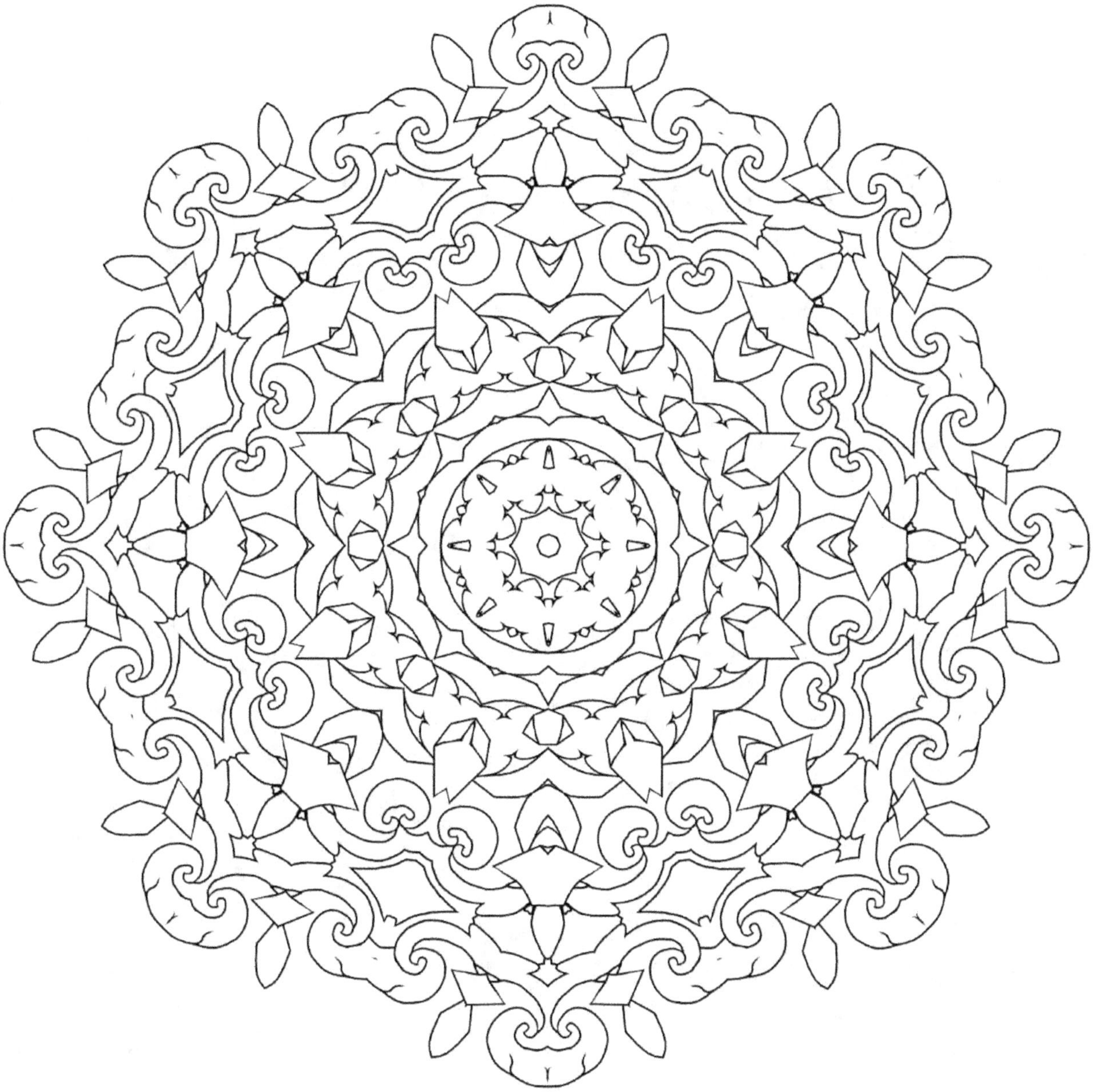

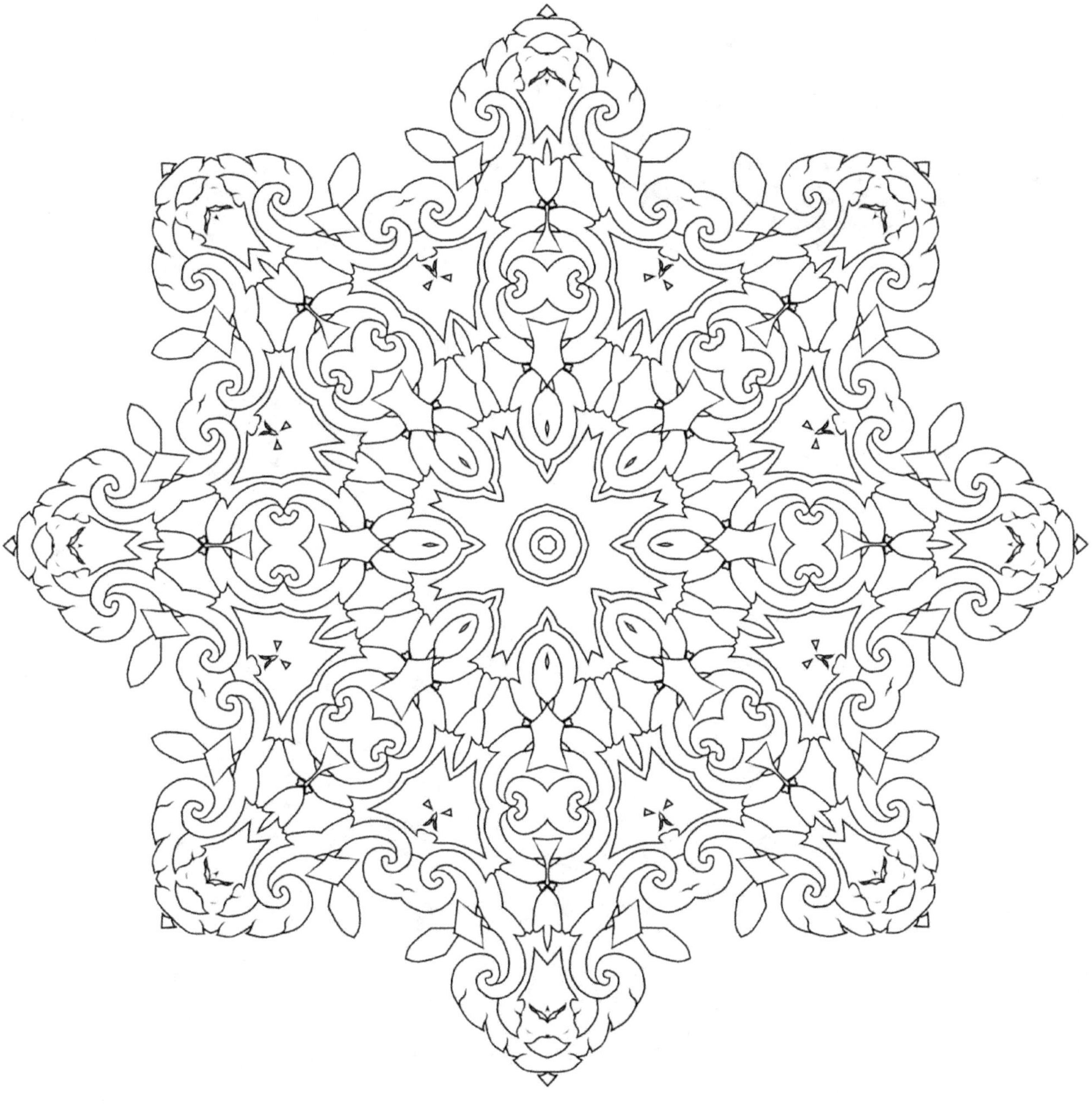

Thank you

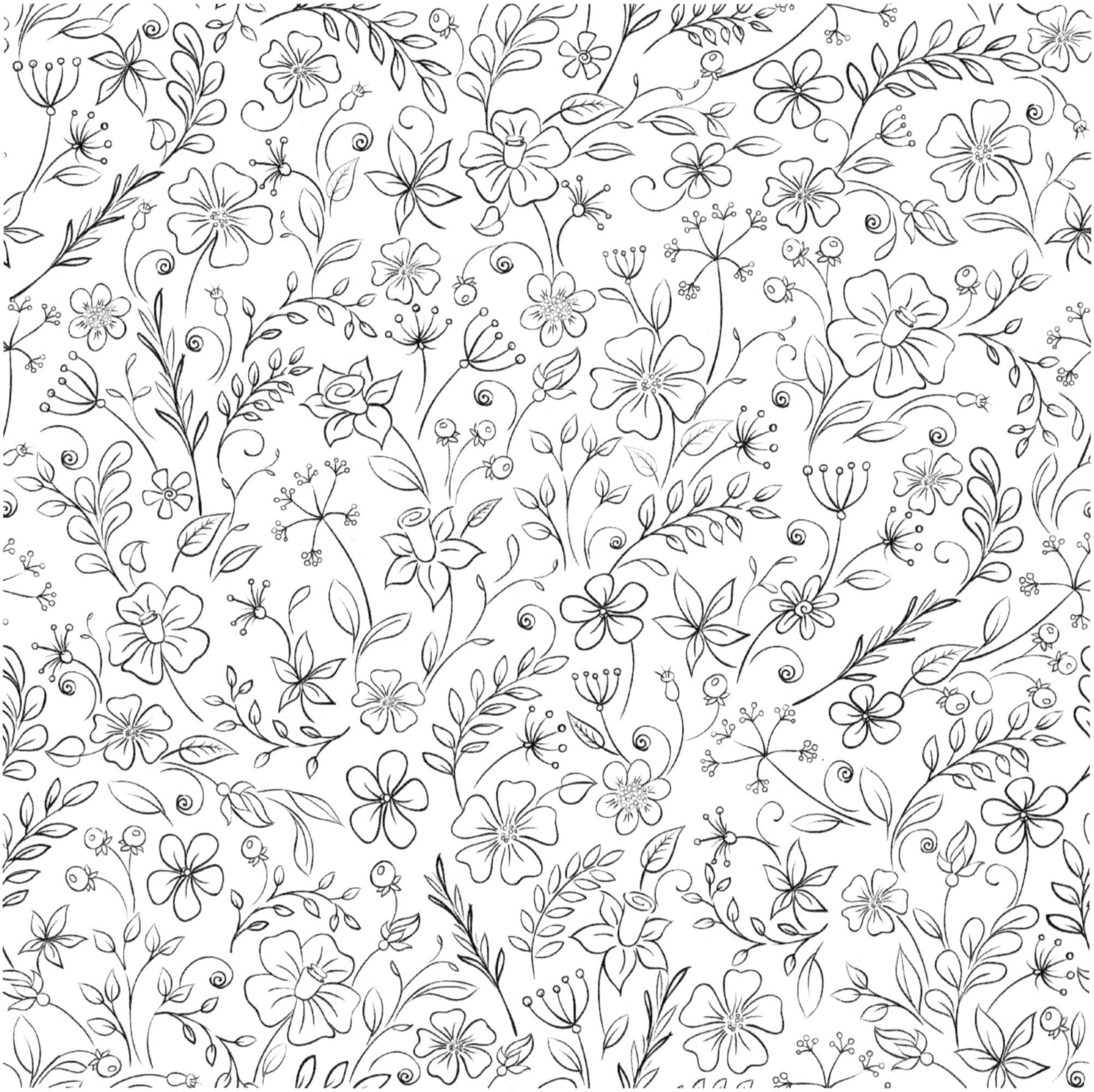

www.ingramcontent.com/pod-product-compliance
Lightning Source LLC
Chambersburg PA
CBHW081117180526
45170CB00008B/2891
* 9 7 8 1 5 4 2 6 4 2 0 0 2 *